The African Department

CW01574903

Private Finance for Development

Wishful Thinking or Thinking Out of the Box?

Prepared by an IMF staff team led by Luc Eyraud and comprised of
Hilary Devine, Adrian Peralta Alva, Hoda Selim,
Preya Sharma, and Ludger Wocken

INTERNATIONAL MONETARY FUND

Cataloging-in-Publication Data
IMF Library

Names: Eyraud, Luc. | Devine, Hilary. | Peralta Alva, Adrian. | Selim, Hoda. | Sharma, Preya. | Wocken, Ludger. | International Monetary Fund. African Department, issuing body. | International Monetary Fund, publisher.

Title: Private finance for development : wishful thinking or thinking out of the box? / prepared by an IMF staff team led by Luc Eyraud and comprised of Hilary Devine, Adrian Peralta Alva, Hoda Selim, Preya Sharma, and Ludger Wocken.

Other titles: International Monetary Fund. African Department (Series).

Description: Washington, DC : International Monetary Fund, 2021. | Departmental paper series. | Includes bibliographical references.

Identifiers: ISBN 9781513571560 (paper)

Subjects: LCSH: Public-private sector cooperation—Africa. | Infrastructure (Economics)—Africa.| Economic development—Africa.

Classification: LCC HD3872.A35 E97 2021

Publication orders may be placed online, by fax, or through the mail:
International Monetary Fund, Publication Services
P.O. Box 92780, Washington, DC 20090, U.S.A.
Tel. (202) 623-7430 Fax: (202) 623-7201
E-mail: publications@imf.org
www.imfbookstore.org
www.elibrary.imf.org

Contents

Boxes

Acknowledgments

This paper was written by a staff team led by Luc Eyraud, and composed of Hilary Devine, Adrian Peralta Alva, Hoda Selim, Preya Sharma, and Ludger Wocken (all from the African Department at the time of writing). Mauricio Soto provided useful contributions at an early stage of the project. Zarina Bentum provided excellent research assistance. Nadia Margevich and Amparo Gamboa Gonzalez were responsible for document production. The authors have received overall guidance from Catherine Pattillo, Abebe Selassie, and Zeine Zeidane. They gratefully acknowledge the valuable comments and inputs provided by Luc Albinski, Isabell Adenauer, Olusegun Akanbi, Angham al Shami, Vivek Arora, Paul Austin, Tonci Bakovic, Lars Bane, Stephen Bailey-Smith, Bryn Battersby, Pasquale Di Benedetta, Houda Berrada, Mohamed Camara, Guillaume Chabert, Hua Chai, Omar Chaudry, Paul Collier, Mattia Coppo, Saha Deblina, Sage de Clerck, Kawtar Eddahmani, Annalisa Fedelino, Nicoletta Feruglio, Michael Fuchs, Fabien Gonguet, Simon Gray, Francesco Grigoli, Daniel Gurara, Tunc Gursoy, Mona Haddad, Zhi Yong Heng, Jiro Honda, Seong Ho Hong, Thordur Jonasson, Andrew Kanyegirire, Vitaliy Kramarenko, Ivo Krznar, Bertrand Heysch de la Borde, Hans-Peter Lankes, Sebastien Leduc, Darius Lilaoonwala, Rodolfo Maino, Aurelie Martin, Silvia Matei, Tilla McAntony, Soline Miniere, Teshura Sharmila Nair, Sundeep Naran, Michel Noel, Neree Noumon, Emmanuel Nyirinkindi, David Owen, Lorena Rivero del Paso, Catriona Purfield, Sandeep Saxena, Alasdair Scott, Elena Sterlin, Philip Stokoe, Xin Tang, Vimal Thakoor, Alexander Tieman, Menexenia Tsaroucha, Marcos Vaena, Vivien Foster, Alexei Volkov, Yuan Xiao, Jeromin Zettelmeyer, Yuanyan Sophia Zhang, and other IMF colleagues.

Executive Summary

Does Africa need more private finance? The COVID-19 pandemic has aggravated the tension between large development needs in infrastructure and scarce public resources. To alleviate this tension and promote a strong and job-rich recovery from the crisis, Africa needs to mobilize more financing from and to the private sector.

Why now? It is a pivotal moment for Africa. In recent years, many African countries have relied on public investment-driven growth, which is reaching its limits given high debt levels and limited domestic revenue mobilization. Moreover, the pandemic has eroded the foundations on which progress was achieved in the past two decades (strong global growth, easy access to external financing, supportive commodity prices). In this new environment, development strategies need a rethink.

Is this time different? Developing countries have already experienced a wave of private sector participation in infrastructure in the 1990s. Results were disappointing, which undermined public confidence and support, and the experiment was later reversed. Lessons have been learned from this episode to make private sector delivery of infrastructure services more sustainable, both economically and socially.

How much could the private sector contribute to meeting development spending needs? Historical evidence shows that the private sector takes increasing responsibilities in the provision and financing of infrastructure as countries move up the income ladder. The paper estimates that private finance could bring an additional 3 percent of GDP in African countries over the next decade, equally split between domestic and international investors. Going beyond this figure would require active policies to attract new types of private finance flows (foreign institutional investors and philanthropy), above and beyond historical patterns.

Where does the continent start from? At the moment, the contribution of the private sector to financing social and physical infrastructure is very limited in Africa, given the needs and compared to other regions. Nearly all infrastructure projects are carried out by the public sector. And even sectors with strong private participation tend to be heavily reliant on financial support (cofinancing and guarantees) provided by governments and international development institutions.

Why has private finance in Africa been low? Risk-adjusted returns of private projects in Africa are perceived by financial investors as less attractive than elsewhere in the world, especially in the past decade. This is primarily due to two factors: (1) market failures and Africa-specific factors that limit private returns in development sectors and (2) elevated investment risks that crystalize more specifically around poor project preparation, high exchange-rate risk, and difficulties in divesting.

What role should the government play to attract private finance in social and physical infrastructure? This departmental paper proposes a three-pronged approach to address the main bottlenecks to greater private sector involvement, articulated around the concepts of risk mitigation, promotion, and compensation.

- *Risk mitigation.* With the assistance of the international community, governments need to continue to strengthen the business climate to lower project, macroeconomic, and exit risks—three key concerns for investors.
- *Promotion.* Market failures are prevalent in development sectors, calling for actions that go beyond business climate improvements. Experience shows that about half of the infrastructure projects with private participation in Africa get some form of public support. Although their track record is uneven, targeted government incentives (subsidies and guarantees) may be necessary to attract financial investors and ensure that projects come through. Incentives must be carefully designed to make their use more effective and efficient.
- *Compensation.* Measures need to be in place to accompany the economic actors negatively impacted by pro-business reforms, in particular poor households that may see the cost of utilities and other services go up. In the past, many private sector participation reforms have been derailed by the lack of social consensus and the inability to share reform gains broadly within the population.

Will it be expensive for the government? Yes, both financially and politically. Countries have to face the reality that infrastructure services must be paid for, whether their provision is public or private. These services are not free or cheap, and even when the private sector is involved, significant costs remain for the government. The good news is that, when public incentives are well-designed, public funds can have a multiplier effect on the quantity and quality of infrastructure services. This multiplier is unlikely to be high enough to turn "billions into trillions of dollars" but even moderate multipliers could motivate some reallocation of public funds from traditional public investment toward incentives for private investment. This could be particularly useful in sectors with a poor track record of public provision, where low-quality infrastructure services are delivered by loss-making and inefficient state-owned enterprises.

Can these costs be reduced? Yes, to some extent. There is scope to shift part of the costs associated with mitigation/promotion/compensation from the government to other entities. The blending paradigm proposes to use donors' money to catalyze private finance, although its implementation and possible extension raises many practical issues. A similar framework could be considered with philanthropic resources (foundations and high-wealth individuals), with a view to developing a partnership between businesses, philanthropic actors, and governments in development sectors.

Is this private finance model applicable to all African countries? The balance between public and private finance needs to pay heed to the country context. Countries with relatively strong state capacity and institutions, already at or close to middle-income level, and with market access, are more attractive to international investors and could benefit significantly from programs meant to mobilize and incentivize private finance. For smaller low-income countries, with weaker capacity and possibly higher needs (as a share of their economy), the priority should be to enhance the efficiency of public investment and attract more official aid, which is too often skewed toward richer and more stable countries.

Chapter 1 Introduction and General Framework

To fulfill their development agenda and promote a strong recovery from the COVID-19 crisis, sub-Saharan African countries will have to carry out substantial investments in physical infrastructure, education, and healthcare in the coming years. In a context of stretched public finances, success will depend crucially on their ability to mobilize more financing for private projects.

Large Development Gaps in Africa . . .

Over the past two decades, development outcomes have improved significantly in sub-Saharan Africa (SSA). SSA countries have made continuous progress in the eight UN Millennium Development Goals (MDGs) set in 2000. Between the late 1990s and 2019, real per capita income rose by about 40–50 percent on average in the region; poverty headcount rates fell from about 60 percent to about 40 percent; school enrollment rates increased to 70 percent; infant mortality rates fell from about 100 to about 50 per 1,000 live births. These achievements have been the result of various factors, including policy reforms, relatively high commodity prices, favorable global financial conditions, and the fiscal space created by the Heavily Indebted Poor Countries Initiative and Multilateral Debt Relief Initiative (HIPC/MDRI).

However, the region still faces significant gaps. Building on the progress achieved under the MDGs, new development objectives were set by the United Nations in 2015, with 17 UN Sustainable Development Goals (SDGs) setting a roadmap toward more inclusive growth. As of today, most SSA countries remain far away from the SDG targets. The median composite SDG index score—a measure that tracks performance across all SDG areas—is about 50 percent in SSA (Figure 1). In contrast, the emerging market economies (EMEs) and advanced economies (AEs) are much closer to the targets as their median scores are 66 and 78 percent, respectively. Fur-

Figure 1. Regional SDG Global Index Scores
(Percent)

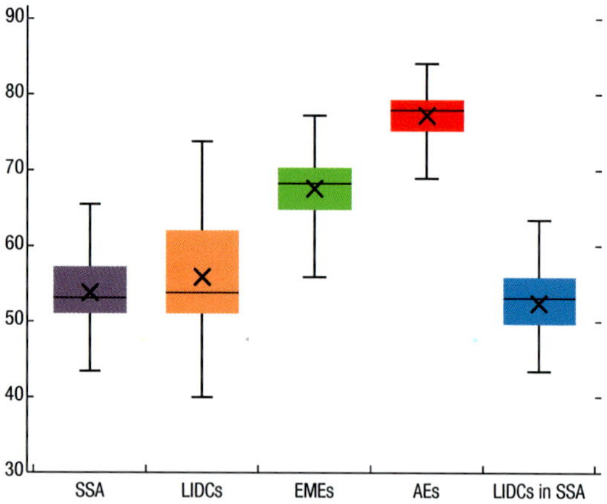

Sources: 2019 SDG Index and Dashboards; and IMF staff calculations.
Note: Line inside the box indicates the median value, and the marker indicates the average value. SSA = sub-Saharan Africa; LIDCs = low-income developing countries; EMEs = emerging market economies; AEs = Advanced economies; LIDCs in SSA = low-income developing countries in sub-Saharan Africa.

Figure 2. Sub-Saharan Africa: Real GDP per Capita, 2000–20
(Index 2000 = 100)

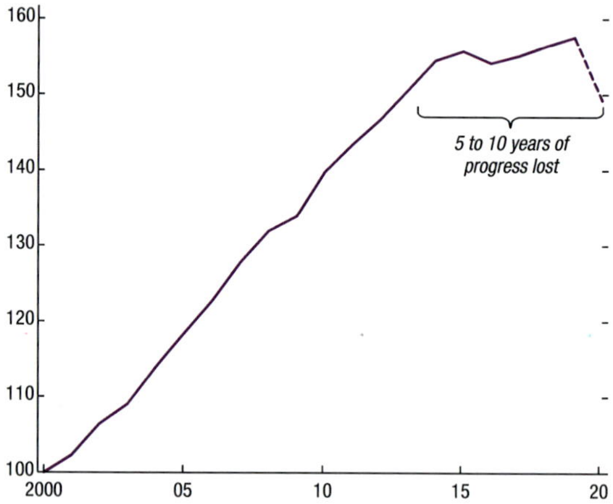

Source: IMF, *World Economic Outlook* database.

thermore, the variation in SDG scores is somewhat larger within low-income developing countries than within other income groups.

And the COVID-19 pandemic constitutes an unprecedented threat to development. Africa is facing one of the most serious health and economic crises of its history. The crisis threatens to throw the region off its stride, reversing the economic and social progress of recent years. In 2020, the SSA region is projected to see its worst growth outcome since 1970, with a sizeable decline in per capita incomes (Figure 2). The containment measures, which are central to limiting the spread of the virus, have incapacitated the informal economy, which ranges 20–65 percent of GDP across Africa and typically helps cushion the blow to livelihoods during downturns. As a result, millions are being pushed into extreme poverty, and the region is likely to witness its first increase in poverty rates in nearly two decades. Moreover, as the health crisis wanes, countries will likely resort to cuts in physical and social expenditure to restore fiscal sustainability, making SDG attainment much more difficult.

. . . And Shrinking Public Resources to Finance Them

Public resources are limited compared to the scale of the development needs. Before the COVID-19 crisis, SSA countries had already experienced a pronounced rise in sovereign debt, with average public debt increasing by almost 25 percentage points during 2010–19 (Figure 3; IMF 2019b). In parallel, the capacity to service debt had deteriorated sharply, with the average inter-

Figure 3. Sub-Saharan Africa: Total Public Debt, 2000–20
(Percent of GDP, weighted average)

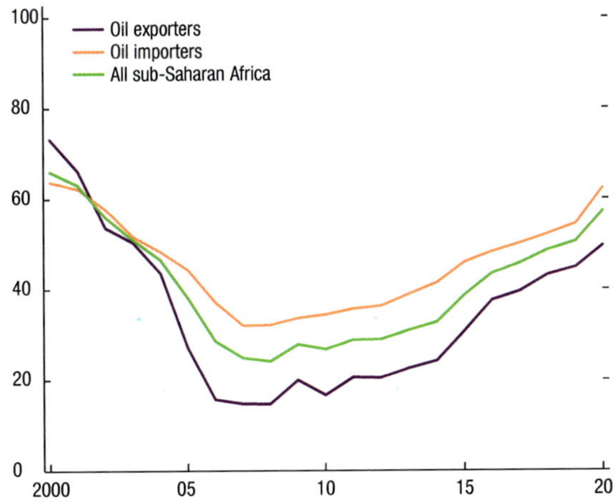

Sources: IMF, *World Economic Outlook*.

Figure 4. Net Official Development Assistance Received by Sub-Saharan African Countries, 1990–2018
(Percent of SSA GDP)

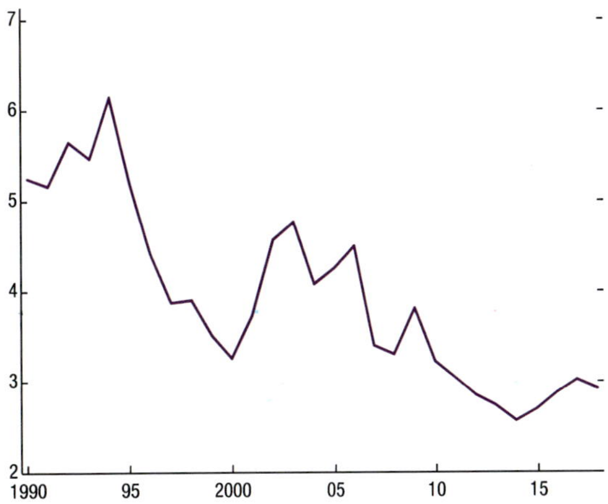

Sources: World Bank Development Indicators; OECD Development Assistance Committee; and IMF staff calculations.

est payments-to-revenue (including grants) ratio doubling from 5 percent in 2010 to 11 percent in 2019. The increase in the debt and interest ratios was most pronounced among oil exporters. 16 out of 35 SSA LICs were at high risk of or in debt distress in 2019. In addition, the public debt increase has taken place in a context of stagnating, or even declining, official development assistance in recent years. Net official development assistance (ODA) received by SSA countries has dropped by more than 3 percentage points of GDP since its peak in the mid-1990s (Figure 4).[1]

With the COVID-19 crisis, what little fiscal space African economies had has shrunk further and will be very difficult to recoup over the next few years. The crisis has led to significant contractions in domestic revenues and access to global financial markets at a time when expenditures on health and income support have increased. For the region as a whole, preliminary estimates suggest that the aggregate debt ratio increased from 50.4 percent of GDP in 2019 to 56.6 percent of GDP in 2020. In addition, the crisis has generated persistent fiscal pressures that are unlikely to dissipate soon. Some of the measures introduced during the crisis to support vulnerable populations and strengthen the healthcare system will be very difficult to withdraw, even those that were designed as temporary, while revenue mobilization

[1]The official aid variable shown in Figure 4 comes from the OECD Development Assistance Committee (DAC) statistics. Since China is not a member of the DAC, Chinese investments in Africa are not formally characterized as ODA, but can nonetheless contain concessional elements akin to ODA. In the absence of publicly available data on Chinese investments, it is not possible to correct the official aid series, but one has to keep in mind that Figure 4 may overestimate the decline in official aid.

efforts may durably be hampered by the economic disruptions brought by the crisis. As a result, the financing required to scale-up pro-poor spending to achieve the SDGs, which was already large before the crisis, is likely to become an even bigger challenge.

Role and Definition of Private Finance

The private sector is viewed increasingly as a key partner to meet Africa's large development needs in the medium to long term. Billions of dollars are needed to support economic development in Africa, address the costly infrastructure gaps, and promote a job-rich recovery from the COVID-19-induced downturn. This ambitious objective cannot be achieved solely by tapping upon traditional public financing sources. A large part of the additional investment and financing will need to come from the private sector. Catalyzing private finance to foster inclusive growth is at the core of development models promoted by several international institutions as well as international initiative such as the Compact with Africa (AfDB, IMF, and WBG 2017).

The private sector can intervene in development sectors in several ways. The term "private finance" is commonly used to describe the role of the private sector as fund provider and/or recipient. The literature uses other terms, such as "private sector participation" or "public-private partnerships", which have a broader meaning, covering also project implementation, not just financing.

This paper uses the term "private finance" to characterize the financing flows going to private service producers. Under the private finance scheme, financial investors either lend to or take equity stakes in development projects that are *not* controlled by the government (left side of Figure 5). The service producer—for example, a hospital or a power plant—is assumed to be a private market producer; its liabilities are not recorded as liabilities of the general government.[2] Therefore, private finance flows do not increase government debt, but create, in general, private sector liabilities.[3] It is worth emphasizing that the term "private finance" is defined in this paper by the sectorization of the entity receiving the financing, not the entity providing the financing. For instance, a private household buying a government bond is considered a form of "public finance." On the other hand, Development

[2]A "market producer" is an entity that sells its services at prices that are economically significant (but prices do not need to fully cover costs). The "general government" comprises all government units of central, state, provincial, regional, and local government, and social security funds, as well as all nonmarket nonprofit institutions that are controlled by government units. See the IMF *Government Finance Statistics Manual 2014* for more information on statistical sectorization.

[3]Philanthropic flows going to the private sector are an exception, since they do not generate private sector liabilities for the recipient. But all other types of financial flows (equity and debt) do.

Figure 5. Private and Public Finance Schemes

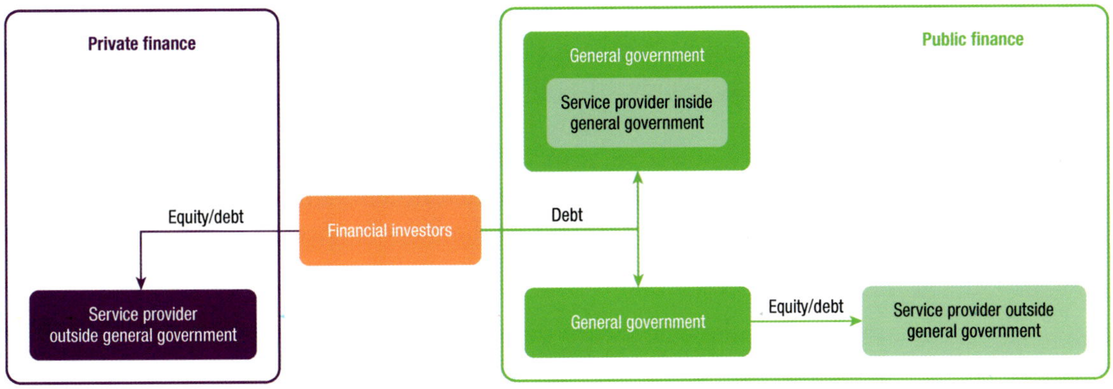

Source: IMF staff.

Finance Institutions (both bilateral and multilateral) investing in private projects are considered a form of "private finance," since such operations do not impact directly national governments' balance sheets.

By contrast, this paper uses the term "public finance" to refer to arrangements where development projects are financed directly or indirectly by the government, thereby impacting the public balance sheet. The government can either provide services directly (with a line ministry in charge of the implementation) or finance a service provider outside the general government, such as a private corporation or a state-owned enterprises (SOE) (Figure 5, right side). Either way, when the government borrows to conduct such activities, government debt increases. Such funding models are defined as "public finance."

Many financing schemes considered in this paper lie between the two polar cases of pure private finance and pure public finance. Public-private partnerships and other forms of financial collaborations between government and private entities, which are widespread in the field of infrastructure financing, may impact the liabilities of both sectors.[4] And the degree of private sector participation, including its financial involvement, can vary significantly across projects and across legal arrangements (see discussion in Chapter 4).

There is also a grey area around the perimeter of "public finance." Some service producers, like SOEs, fulfil a public function but are, statistically

[4]From a purely statistical standpoint, the IMF *Government Finance Statistics Manual 2014* does not recommend splitting a public-private partnership (PPP) arrangement between public and private financing, but rather looks at the entity as a whole to be either inside or outside of the general government sector. This determination is based on the economic ownership of the underlying asset involved in the PPP arrangement. Should that economic ownership be determined to be the government, then the whole of the PPP unit will be classified inside the general government sector and its liabilities will be public. Should it be determined that the underlying asset's economic owner is the private party, then the whole of the entity will be recorded as belonging to the private sector.

speaking, outside the general government sector. From a statistical point of view, SOE debt is not government debt but it is not private debt either; it should be recorded as "public sector" liability, although African countries do not produce consolidated public sector statistics. This paper considers the financing of SOEs operating in development sectors as a form of public finance, since the objective of involving the private sector is to generate new financial resources, not to shift some investments from the balance sheet of the narrowly defined government to the balance sheet of entities within the broader public sector.

In practice, the choice between private finance and public finance depends on efficiency, equity, and feasibility considerations. This paper argues that there is scope for increasing the contribution of private finance in SSA, in particular from international sources. But the ultimate objective is not to reallocate all savings from the public to the private sector. The desired level of private involvement depends on the characteristics of the country, the development sector and even the project, as discussed in Chapter 4. A key consideration is the relative size of private versus social returns, with projects generating high private returns more likely to attract private finance (Annex 1). The choice between public and private financing depends also on the efficient allocation of risks, with financing expected to go to the party most capable of managing the risks associated with the project; any attempt to transfer risks and controls in excess of what is optimal could lead to inefficient utilization of capital and higher project costs (see Chapter 5). Another consideration is financial sustainability: if either the private or the public sector is overleveraged and at high risk of debt distress, its ability to borrow and invest in new projects is clearly more limited. Finally, equity and inclusiveness are very important factors for sustainable development; they can tilt the balance toward public finance when the private sector is not willing to or capable of ensuring universal access to basic services.

Scope and Structure of the Paper

This paper examines whether it is desirable and possible to mobilize more finance for private or semi-private projects in development sectors in Africa. The paper does not cost Africa's development needs, but builds on estimates computed by Gaspar and others (2019) and other sources. It concentrates on five sectors at the core of sustainable and inclusive growth, which cover both physical and social infrastructure: road, power, water, education, and health.[5] The paper focuses on the financing side of development projects, while

[5]Infrastructure is defined as long-term physical assets that enable the provision of (often strategic) goods and services. "Social Infrastructure" is a subset of the infrastructure sector and typically includes assets that accommodate social services, including education and health.

recognizing that it is only one aspect of the challenge. Financing is essential, but it can be wasted where the selection and execution of investment projects are poorly managed. Therefore, progress on the development agenda requires closing both the financing and efficiency gaps. This paper considers the two dimensions, although its main focal point is the financing side.

The paper places more emphasis on the role of international private finance. In principle, the fund providers can be either domestic or foreign entities. The main purpose of this paper is to identify policies that mobilize international finance, although many recommendations apply to domestic investors as well. The development of domestic financial markets has been the subject of a great deal of work, including for Africa (see, for instance, Laeven 2014 or Mlachila and others 2016). In addition, the time horizon for achieving the SDGs (about a decade) is shorter than the time needed to significantly improve the depth, access, and efficiency of local financial markets in Africa.

The geographical coverage of the paper is sub-Saharan Africa (SSA). Although many arguments and considerations discussed in this paper are relevant for the whole African continent as well as other developing countries,[6] the paper concentrates on the SSA region, which comprises 45 countries (see list in the IMF *Regional Economic Outlook: Sub-Saharan Africa* publications). SSA lags behind other regions in terms of development outcomes and infrastructure gaps, despite some progress in the past two decades. The region is home to at least half of the world's poor, has the largest share of fragile countries, and the most acute fiscal and debt sustainability constraints. But it will also account for about one-third of the global labor force by 2050, and with significant investment the region could become a future engine of global growth.

The economic damages and fundamental disruptions caused by the COVID-19 pandemic have made the need for private finance more critical but its potential more uncertain. The pandemic has not only reduced governments' available resources, but also scarred the countries' growth potential, shifted economic structures, and dampened investors' confidence. The private sector has been hit hard by the crisis. It may take a long time for certain industries—contact-intensive service sectors such as transportation and low-skill manufacturing industries—to fully recover. Global risk aversion could remain heightened, restricting the ability to attract foreign funding. The pandemic may also reshape the patterns of international investment flows both in terms of risk preferences as well as sectoral allocation, for instance to digitalized and greener investments. All this creates much uncertainty about

[6]In the paper, the term "developing countries" refers to both low-income developing countries and emerging market economies, as defined in the IMF *World Economic Outlook*. A "developing region" encompasses the developing countries belonging to a given region. For instance, "emerging Europe" is the subset of European countries that are not advanced economies.

the outlook and the effectiveness of traditional policy levers. In this very difficult context, the main recommendations of this paper should be considered with some caution. No simple formula will achieve development objectives, and this paper does not claim that easy or quick solutions will solve the immense challenges faced by African countries in the post-COVID world.

The paper is divided into seven chapters that offer various perspectives on the role of and potential for private finance in SSA. Chapter 2 assesses the need for more private finance in the region. Chapter 3 describes some trends and identifies the main obstacles to attracting financial investors. Chapter 4 highlights reforms and policies for creating a business environment more conducive to private finance. Chapter 5 focuses on the rationale and types of public interventions needed to catalyze private finance. Chapter 6 explores the potential for bringing new investors in development sectors in Africa, such as institutional investors and philanthropic flows. Chapter 7 concludes.

CHAPTER

2 How Much Can Private Finance Contribute to Development Goals in Africa?

Achieving development objectives and promoting a strong recovery from the COVID-19 crisis will require sizeable investments in education, health, and infrastructure over the next decade. Additional financing is critical to making meaningful progress toward these goals. The scale of the needs requires efforts from all stakeholders. African countries should implement ambitious revenue mobilization and expenditure efficiency reforms to create budgetary space for development spending. Support from the international community, including donors and international financial institutions, will also be essential to meeting development spending needs. And the private sector can also do more: this chapter estimates that an ambitious but realistic target is to raise the contribution of private finance in SSA countries by 3 percent of GDP by the end of the decade.

The Scale of Development Needs

Addressing the needs in physical and social infratructure will entail very high costs for African countries. Gaspar and others (2019) estimate the annual spending required for meaningful progress on the SDGs in five key sectors: education, health, roads, electricity, and water and sanitation. Their analysis, conducted before the COVID crisis, finds that meeting the development objectives in these areas will require additional annual spending—both private and public—of $0.5 trillion for low-income developing countries and $2.1 trillion for emerging market economies in 2030. Spending needs vary greatly across countries, with the highest-need economies located in SSA (Figure 6). In this region, additional expenditure accounts on average for about 20 percent of GDP.[1] This figure is above the low-income developing

[1]An update of the costing exercise conducted internally by the IMF Fiscal Affairs Department at the end of 2020 (based on 2018 data) did not find major revisions compared to Gaspar and others (2019), which was based on 2017 data. The median expenditure needs across SSA countries continue to be estimated at about 20 percent of GDP.

Figure 6. Additional Spending Needs in 2030 by Country
(Percent of GDP; sample of low-income developing countries and emerging market economies)

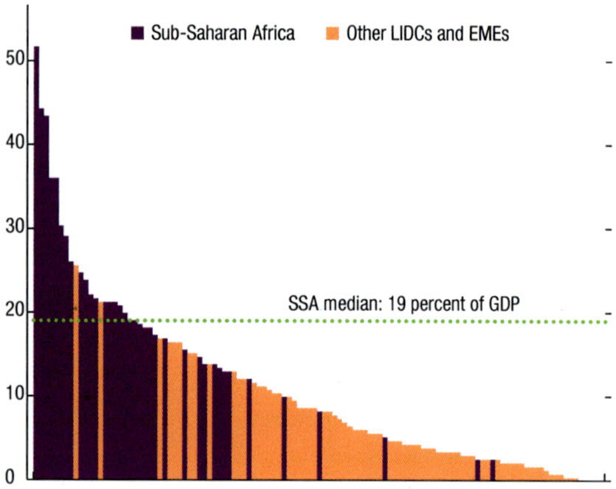

Source: Gaspar and others (2019).
Note: EMEs = emerging market economies; LIDCs = low-income developing countries; SSA = sub-Saharan Africa.

Figure 7. Sub-Saharan Africa: Composition of Additional Spending Needs in 2030
(Percent of GDP)

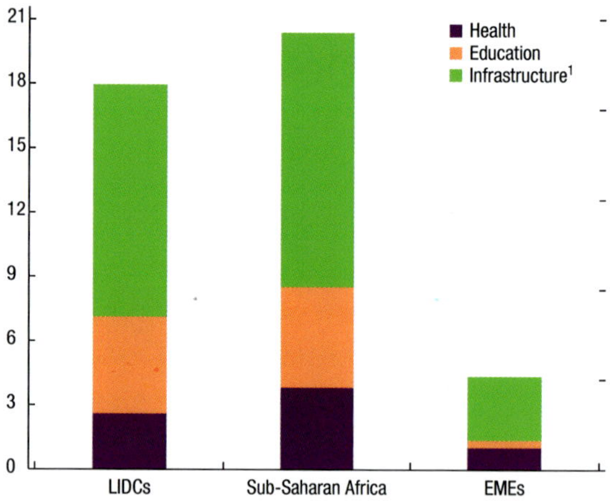

Source: Gaspar and others (2019).
Note: Bars represent simple averages across countries in each group.
[1]Infrastructure includes electricity, roads, water, and sanitation.

country (LIDC) average, primarily because of higher physical infrastructure needs in SSA (Figure 7).

These additional costs, which could be split between the private and public sectors, are expected to be recurrent. It is important to clarify two potential misunderstandings regarding the interpretation of the SDG costing estimates. First, additional spending needs are computed for the year 2030, which is the time horizon of the SDGs; however, these costs would be recurrent. This means that to close the development gaps, expenditure should be higher in 2030 but also in subsequent years (although the exact estimate of additional needs in, say, 2032 may differ somewhat from the 2030 figure due to several factors, including changes in demographics and maintenance costs of infrastructure). Second, the costing exercise is agnostic about whether the additional services (for example, roads) should be provided by the private or the public sector. Thus, there is no reason to assume that the additional costs will be borne entirely by governments.

There are also large development gaps outside physical and social infrastructure. The estimates provided by Gaspar and others (2019) focus on five sectors and, thus, do not cover all aspects of development. For instance, costs associated with climate adaptation for SSA are estimated at $30–50 billion (2–3 percent of regional GDP) each year over the next decade (IMF 2020). Affordable, quality, and universal broadband connectivity in SSA adds another $9 billion annually (Broadband Commission 2019). Economic diversification away from traditional and commodity-oriented sectors is another important development objective, although more difficult to cost (IMF 2017).

The COVID-19 crisis is likely to make the needs even larger. Although it is still too early to precisely assess the impact of the pandemic, the crisis does risk setting back previous achievements in human and social development, particularly in the areas of health, school enrollment, life expectancy, and poverty reduction. The pandemic also has highlighted underlying weaknesses in African countries' public institutions and infrastructures, such as limited social safety nets to adequately protect those at higher risk of falling into poverty and uneven access to quality public services by different groups in the population. The situation could worsen in the coming years if countries resort to cuts in social expenditure and public investment to preserve debt sustainability.

Mobilizing More Resources from All Stakeholders

The scale of the needs will require significant efforts from all stakeholders. Financing development calls for cooperation at the global level. The following paragraphs examine briefly the potential from various sources of financing, which are both domestic and international. The discussion focuses on the big picture and provides broad orders of magnitude for the contributions of all parties by 2030. A more sophisticated and country-specific approach, relying on a dynamic macroeconomic framework to assess development strategies and their financing, is proposed by Benedek and others (2021).

The responsibility to generate additional resources for development lies first with African countries themselves. Domestic reforms range from strengthening macroeconomic management to boosting government revenue and implementing more effective spending plans:

- Raising more tax revenues is a central component of the strategy to meet the SDGs. IMF (2018c), Akitoby and others (2019), and Gaspar and others (2019) deem that increasing the tax-to-GDP ratio by 5 percentage points of GDP over the next decade is an ambitious but realistic target for many low-income countries. The more recent analysis by Benedek and others (2021), which takes into account COVID-19 crisis developments, sets a target of 3–7 percent of GDP for comprehensive tax strategies in developing countries. This could be achieved through a combination of reforms that improve the design of tax systems (including the elimination of tax preferences), strengthen the capacity of national revenue administrations, and build public support to enhance tax compliance (IMF 2018b).

- Raising government spending efficiency could generate savings, creating budgetary space for priority programs. Efficiency measures would also reduce financing needs by achieving broadly similar outcomes at a lower cost. A conservative estimate, based on efficiency frontier calculation (set by best performers in LIDCs and emerging market economies), shows that SSA countries could generate about 2–3 percent of GDP of savings in this area.
- The scope for further government borrowing seems more limited, however. Nearly half of low-income countries in SSA were in or at high risk of debt distress at the end of 2020, according to the IMF-World Bank debt sustainability analysis. As discussed in Chapter 1, debt ratios have increased very significantly in the past decade in most countries of the region and are expected to rise even further during the COVID-19 crisis. Therefore, room for additional net borrowing in the medium term has become very thin.[2] Most SSA countries will need to adopt a cautious debt management strategy in the coming years.

If advanced economies delivered on their development assistance targets, the scaling-up of official aid would make a significant contribution toward meeting development spending needs. Resources provided by the international community, including bilateral donors and international financial institutions, are critical to supporting the development efforts of African countries. In 2019 ODA provided by the members of the OECD Development Assistance Committee amounted to only 0.3 percent of their gross national income, with about one-quarter of the funds going to SSA countries. Delivering on ODA targets (0.7 percent of gross national income commitments annually) or better targeting the existing aid envelope toward the poorest countries could generate considerable resources for the SSA region—estimated at 4–5 percent of GDP for a median SSA country.[3]

Private finance has also an important role to play in development sectors. Even in the most optimistic scenario where public resources, including official aid, would be significantly scaled up, large unfunded development needs would remain at the 2030 horizon. This means that the contribution of the private sector will be essential to making meaningful progress toward the SDGs. For most SSA countries, there is room to involve and engage better with the private sector in infrastructure and other development sectors. While possible, this is no easy task. The rest of the paper discusses various policy measures for building an investment-friendly environment and enhancing the

[2]"Net borrowing," which refers to borrowing beyond and above simple debt rollover, results in a debt stock increase.

[3]The 0.7 percent ODA target (expressed in percent of donors' national income) was set by a United Nations General Assembly resolution in 1970. Since then, many advanced economies have pledged to move toward it.

effectiveness of partnerships among private investors, governments, and the international community.

The Potential of Private Finance

To assess the scope for more private finance in SSA, this section analyzes private investment trends across countries and over time. Although the paper focuses on the international contribution of private finance, the analysis of financing should start at the aggregated level, since development needs can be covered by both domestic and international investors. In the absence of a comprehensive, lengthy dataset on private finance flows, this section relies predominantly on national accounts data. In the national accounts, the series of "private investment" describes the expenditure on fixed capital goods carried out by the private sector. The advantage of the series is that it records both domestically and externally financed expenditure. Thus, private investment can be considered as a proxy for the total amount of financing that is raised for private projects. Given that the private sector can self-finance its investment (from revenues generated by the project or retained earnings) and that financing can be used to repay debt or accumulate financial assets, the amount of money spent does not necessarily correspond to the amount of money levied from financial investors in each period. Nonetheless, over a relatively long period of time, the cumulative discrepancy between the two series should not be too large.[4]

Private investment in SSA is on the rise but remains lower than in other developing regions. The private investment-to-GDP ratio of SSA countries increased, on average, from 10.4 percent of GDP in 1990 to 13.5 percent of GDP in 2017, the last year for which data from the IMF investment database is available (Figure 8).[5] Using medians, the increase is more pronounced (4.3 percentage points), reflecting the significant dispersion of country experiences. In fact, the ratio has risen quite impressively in several countries, such as Ethiopia, Ghana, and Tanzania, among others. Yet the median SSA ratio remains lower than in most other developing regions, especially Asia where private investment was close to 16.7 percent of GDP in 2017 (Figure 9; IMF 2018a).

[4]Other limitations of the private investment indicator include the fact that (1) it may include fixed asset formation in sectors with low development spillovers, such as mining activities and (2) it is computed as a residual by deducting government investment from total investment, which means that SOE investment is recorded as private investment. The first issue is examined in Annex 2. The second problem, common to all databases that measure private investment (such as the OECD Analytical Database and the Penn World Tables), is acknowledged but cannot be addressed using existing data sets.

[5]Data used in this section are derived from the IMF "Investment and Capital Stock Dataset, 2019 Update" available at https://infrastructuregovern.imf.org/content/PIMA/Home/PimaTool.html

Figure 8. Sub-Saharan Africa: Private Investment Ratio, 1990 and 2017
(Percent of GDP)

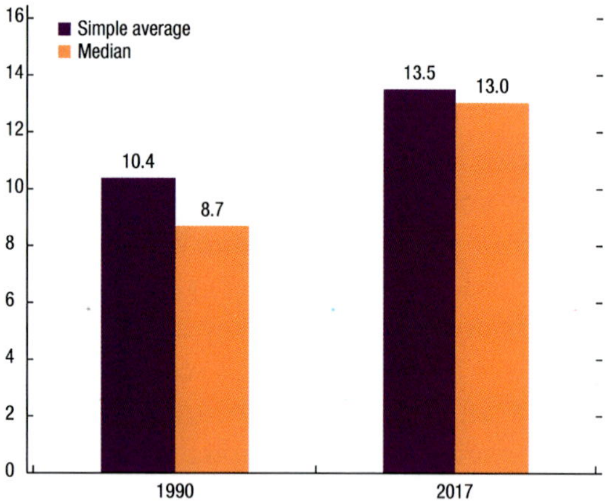

Source: IMF staff calculations based on IMF Investment and Capital Stock Dataset, 2019.

Figure 9. Median Private Investment Ratios by Developing Region, 1990 and 2017
(Percent of GDP)

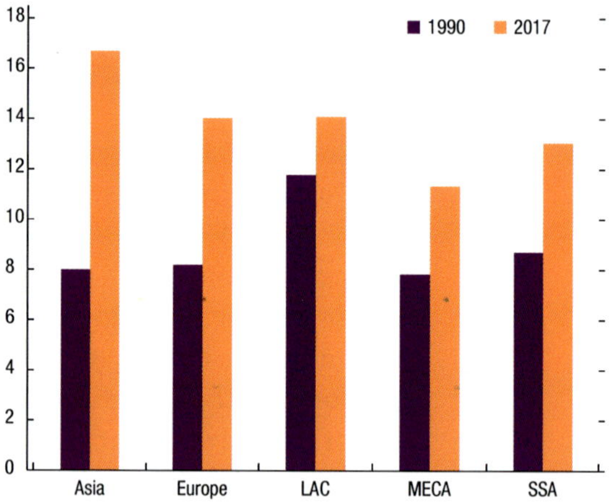

Source: IMF staff calculations based on IMF Investment and Capital Stock Dataset, 2019.
Note: LAC = Latin America and the Caribbean; MECA = Middle East and Central Asia; SSA = sub-Saharan Africa.

And most infrastructure projects in SSA are carried out by the public sector. Infrastructure investment is a subset of total investment that excludes certain items (for example, equipment and residential buildings) as well as rolling expenditure (not made on a project-by-project basis). In 2017 the World Bank published a comprehensive survey of infrastructure investment, combining data from its Private Participation in Infrastructure (PPI) database with a new data set on public projects (World Bank 2017c). The study found that 95 percent of infrastructure project investments in SSA were sponsored by government entities and SOEs in 2017.[6] This means that private projects represented only 5 percent of total investment in infrastructure in the region, compared to an average of 17 percent in low- and middle-income countries (and 40 percent for Latin America—the region with the highest degree of private sector participation). Ghana was an outlier in SSA, recording higher private than public investment commitments in 2017.

Private investment tends to increase when countries converge toward higher income levels. Private investment-to-GDP ratios differ substantially across income groups. The median private investment ratio was 13.0 percent of GDP for SSA countries in 2017 (where the median GDP per capita was about $2,000)—well below the ratio in AEs of 18.9 percent of GDP (Figure 10).

[6]In the analysis of World Bank (2017c), projects with more than 80 percent of government or SOE ownership in the project company's shareholding structure are considered to be public (and characterized as being "sponsored by the public sector"), while the other projects—with minimum 20 percent private ownership in the project's company shareholding structure—are classified as private and described as "PPI projects."

Figure 10. Median Private Investment Ratios by Income Group, 2017
(Percent of GDP)

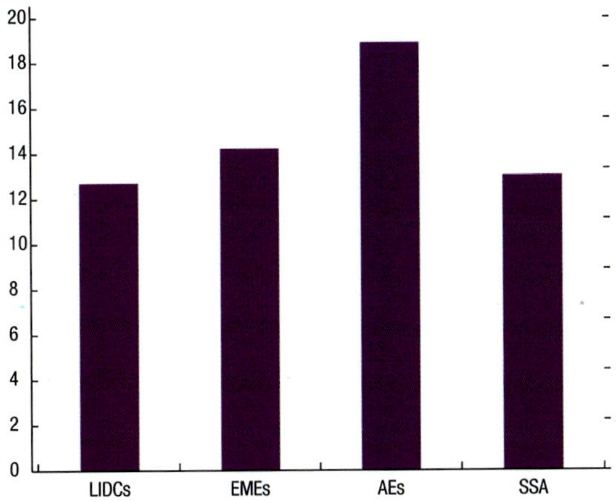

Source: IMF staff calculations based on IMF Investment and Capital Stock Dataset, 2019.

Figure 11. Average Public and Private Investment Ratios by Income Group, 2017
(Percent of GDP)

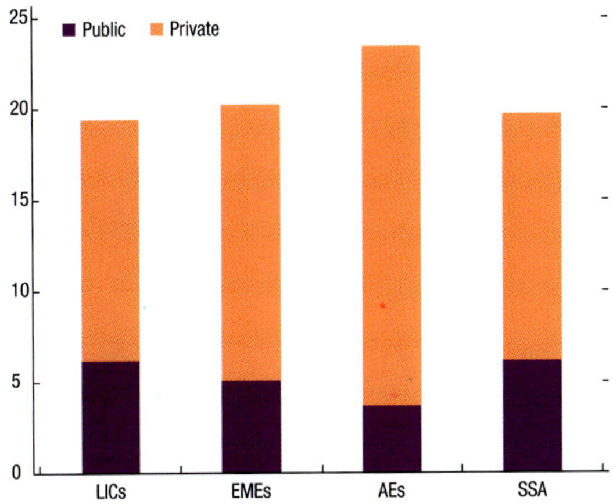

Source: IMF staff calculations based on IMF Investment and Capital Stock Dataset, 2019.

The SSA ratio was close to the median ratio of LIDCs (12.7) and below that of EMEs (14.2), which is not surprising given that the SSA region is mostly composed of LIDCs. The analysis across income groups also shows that the public investment ratio tends to be lower in richer countries, meaning that the composition of investment changes along the income ladder (Figure 11). In 2017 the public investment ratio was almost twice as high in SSA as that in AEs. Overall, these comparisons suggest that there is scope for raising private investment in SSA. But the time horizon of economic development spans over multiple decades. Therefore, it is also important to consider what African countries can realistically accomplish over a shorter period.

Raising private investment in SSA countries by 3 percent of GDP within the next decade seems an achievable goal. Annex 2 reviews country experiences with private investment surges in a global sample since the 1990s. The purpose of the exercise is to identify countries that were able to raise private investment significantly over one decade. The analysis shows that targeting a 3 percent of GDP increase by 2030 is a realistic, though ambitious, target for private investment in SSA countries. A quarter of developing countries (both LIDCs and EMEs) have raised their private investment ratio by more than 3 percent of GDP over the past decade. For SSA, this would broadly correspond to bringing private investment to the 75th percentile median of LIDCs (Figure 12). To go beyond this target, either a longer time horizon should be considered (compared to the 2030 deadline set by the SDGs) or additional sources of private finance should be mobilized, as discussed in Chapter 6. The next section focuses on how the 3 percent of GDP target could be split between domestic and foreign investors.

Figure 12. Median Private Investment Ratio, 2017
(Percent of GDP)

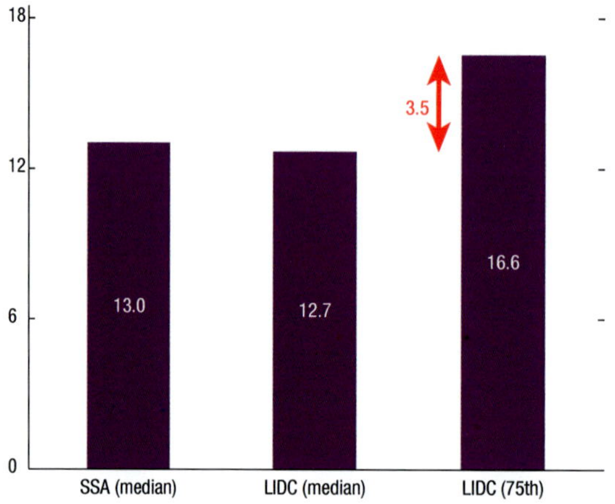

Source: IMF staff calculations based on IMF Investment and Capital Stock Dataset, 2019.

The Contribution of Domestic versus Foreign Investors

In the past decade, about 40 percent of private investment has been financed externally in SSA countries. While the total amount of funding going to the private sector is difficult to estimate, it is even more difficult to get a precise picture of the split between domestic and international financing. A rough estimate can be computed in two steps using several macroeconomic databases. In a first step, the authors compute for each country the amount of external finance going to the private sector by deducting the net incurrence of financial liabilities reported in the IMF Government Finance statistics from the same indicator in the Balance of Payment statistics (which records inflows going to both private and public entities). In a second step, the authors divide the previous series by private investment from the IMF investment database. Excluding outliers, the median split for the financing of private investment in SSA countries was 40 percent external–60 percent domestic during 2010–17 (2017 being the last year with cross-country data available on private investment).

The contribution of international investors is even larger for major infrastructure projects. The World Bank PPI database, which focuses on large infrastructure projects, provides another measure of the composition of financing. It should be noted that this database records infrastructure projects with private participation; therefore, it captures financing flows going to public-private partnerships, which are not purely private projects. During 2011–20, external debt represented, on average, 40 percent of PPI investment in SSA countries. Equity accounted for 30 percent of the investment (see Chapter 3). The rest came mostly from local debt. Available information on the nationality and stakes of individual shareholders, suggests that SSA projects were predominantly sponsored by international investors, with about 70 percent of the projects' equity owned by international entities over the period. Combining debt and equity, this means that about 60 percent of the financing of PPI projects came from foreign investors in SSA. Overall, the estimates using both the macroeconomic databases and the PPI data set suggest that it is reasonable to expect private financing mobilized for achieving the SDGs to be split evenly between domestic and foreign investors.

All in all, this paper estimates that international private finance could increase by, at least, 1½ percent of GDP by the end of the decade. The previous section estimated a target of 3 percent of GDP for the contribution of private finance toward achieving the SDGs by 2030. Assuming equal sharing between domestic and foreign investors, this means that international investors would need to raise their contribution by 1½ percent of GDP by 2030 and maintain it afterward on a sustainable basis. This target is ambitious, since 1½ percent of GDP corresponds to almost 30 percent of today's international financing of private investment in SSA.[7] In other words, international financing of private or semi-private projects in SSA would need to increase by almost a third relative to the current situation.

Progress Requires More Than Just Financing

The mixed track record of the 1990s' private infrastructure boom shows that raising private investment is a matter of quality, not just quantity. Between 1990 and 1998, private sector participation in infrastructure increased very significantly in developing economies, particularly Latin America and East Asia. This episode, which was partly reversed at the end of the decade, had mixed results, in part because the right institutions were not in place to ensure that the involvement of the private sector could be sustained, generate economic and budgetary gains, and translate into clear improvements in standards of living of populations (Box 1).

Lessons were learned from the experience of the 1990s. Although political economy problems remain, some of the institutional weaknesses apparent in the 1990s have been partly addressed or are being addressed, including in Africa. In many areas of infrastructure governance, SSA countries have made significant progress in the past two decades (Barhoumi and others 2018). For instance, most countries have now formal laws or procedures in place

[7]Private investment was estimated at 13 percent of GDP in 2017 (latest year available), out of which 40 percent is estimated to be financed externally. Thus, 1½ percent of GDP is almost 30 percent of international financing (0.4*13 = 5.2).

covering the main elements of the public investment management cycle. Public Investment Management Units have also been established across the region in recent years. The purpose of these units, which are usually located in a country's Ministry of Finance or the Ministry of Planning or Economic Development, is to strengthen the appraisal, selection, and implementation of infrastructure projects.

Several tools have been developed to improve infrastructure governance and better design and implement PPPs. For instance, the Public Investment Management Assessment (PIMA) framework was launched in 2015 to help countries evaluate the institutional design and effectiveness of their infrastructure governance practices across the three key stages of the public investment cycle—planning, allocation, and implementation (IMF 2019d). On PPPs in particular, the PIMA framework recommends a set of good practices to ensure the efficiency of projects, their alignment with development needs, and the management of risks associated with them.[8] As of the end of 2020, 25 SSA countries had undergone a PIMA assessment since 2015. Another analytical tool, the PPP Fiscal Risk Assessment Model (PFRAM) was created to assess the potential fiscal costs and risks arising from individual PPP projects or from PPP portfolios.

[8]The government should, in particular, publish a PPP strategy; adopt a legal framework for the preparation, selection, and management of PPPs; and report the contingent liabilities arising from PPP projects.

Box 1. The 1990s Private Infrastructure Scaling Up

Box Figure 1.1. Total Investment in Infrastructure Projects with Private Participation, 1990–2002
(Billions of US dollars; sample of low- and middle-income economies)

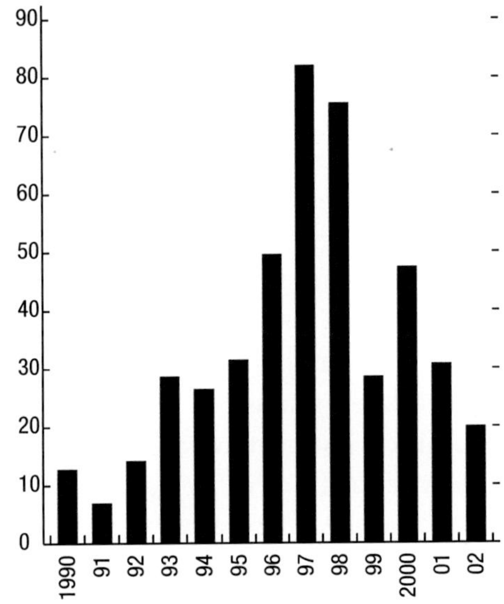

Sources: World Bank Private Participation in Infrastructure Database; and IMF staff calculations.

The 1990s saw a massive increase in private sector participation in infrastructure in developing economies. This shift reflected a combination of factors, including some disappointment with poorly run and inefficient public utilities, governments' budgetary pressures, limited technical and managerial resources in the public sector, successes with pioneer privatization experiences (for example, Chile and the United Kingdom), greater flexibility offered by technological changes (for instance, mobile phone and smaller minimum size for power plants), and regulatory reforms that attract the private sector and oversee its involvement.

According to the World Bank Private Participation in Infrastructure (PPI) database, the nominal value of PPI infrastructure projects (measured on a commitment basis) increased seven-fold between 1990 and 1997–98, with about 1,850 projects and $325 billion of cumulative investment during this period (Box Figure 1.1).[1] As a share of GDP, the value of the annual investment in infrastructure projects with private participation increased by about 1.5 to 2 percent of GDP between 1990 and the peak of 1997–98, depending on the countries' income group (World Bank 2003a). Investments were driven by Latin America and East Asia, mostly in the telecommunication and electricity sectors.

Investment flows peaked in 1997 and then dropped sharply at the end of the decade in the wake of the financial and economic crises in Asia (1997–98) and Argentina (2001–02). This decline was accompanied by renegotiations of projects and some high-profile cancellations. About three-quarters of water and sanitation concessions and half of the transportation concessions in Latin America were renegotiated during

[1]The PPI database records contractual arrangements for medium to large infrastructure projects in which private parties assume operating risks and have at least 20 percent participation in the shareholding structure (World Bank 2017c). The country coverage is low- and middle-income countries. Projects included in the database do not have to be entirely privately owned, financed, or operated. Small projects tend to be omitted because they are usually not reported by the data sources used by the data set.

Box 1. The 1990s Private Infrastructure Scaling Up *(continued)*

the 1990s (Guasch 2004). At the same time, the appetite of private investors waned, reflecting some pessimism about emerging markets' prospects (partly motivated by the strong currency depreciations), concerns over the willingness and ability of governments to fulfil their contractual commitments, and a weakening of the investors' own financial situation. In many countries, public opinion also largely shifted from supporting toward rejecting private sector involvement in the provision of infrastructure services.

The literature has drawn lessons from this episode (see Harris 2003, World Bank 2003a, Andres and others 2008). A consensus seems to emerge that private sector participation did generate substantial welfare gains over the 1990s decade, including greater efficiency, better access and coverage, and improved service quality (reliability, better customer service, more accurate billing, lower waiting time, etc.).

Beyond the conjunctural factors related to the economic crises, the relative failure of and backlash against the new paradigm revealed a number of fundamental weaknesses. First, most contracts were not well designed. For instance, they did not foresee regular review of tariffs or other parameters, requiring any adjustment to be made through renegotiation. Unexpected fiscal costs also emerged because of ill-conceived guarantees and generous risk assignments in the contracts. Second, the political economy of infrastructure pricing proved to be a central concern. Governments in developing countries had a legacy of keeping prices below costs and heavily subsidizing them. Problems emerged when implementing and sustaining tariff reforms, although efficiency gains helped mitigate or even eliminate price increases in the sectors where prices were better aligned with costs like telecommunication and transportation. This challenge proved to be more acute for water and electricity. Third, as a result of the previous two factors, contract renegotiations were frequent, with outcomes generally unfavorable to the users of services (for example, delays, tariff increases, etc.). Fourth, many public utilities were overstaffed, and private participation often led to reductions in the number of employees. Without compensation and support from the state, this led to public discontent.

CHAPTER

3 Private Finance in Africa Today: Stylized Facts and Main Obstacles

Despite the large development needs, capital flows to the SSA region are relatively low and have been volatile in the face of global shocks. Investment flows are not primarily directed to development sectors; rather a large proportion goes to natural resource and extractive industries. The analysis shows that SSA returns are not always sufficient to compensate for the higher risk. Specifically, SSA returns have fallen significantly from a peak in the 2000s, while risks identified by financial investors, including macroeconomic volatility and markets' illiquidity, are perceived to be higher than in other regions and have not diminished markedly over the same period.

Financing Flows to Development Sectors in Africa

Capital inflows to SSA are relatively small and have declined since the mid-2010s.[1] Less than 5 percent of total capital inflows to developing economies—both EMEs and LIDCs—were to SSA in 2019 (Figure 13). Despite many EMEs having benefited from the rise of international financial market integration and globalization, and investors reorienting in search of higher growth and higher yield environment away from AEs after the global financial crisis of 2008, SSA has to some extent been left behind. While there was strong growth in capital inflows to SSA reaching a peak in 2014 of $120 billion fueled in part by commodity prices, since then inflows have declined to $77 billion by 2019. Inflows to the continent are not uniform,

[1]In this section, "capital inflows" are measured as "net incurrent of liabilities" and include foreign direct investment (FDI), portfolio, and other investment flows (the latter category comprise international banks' loans to African projects) taken from the IMF Balance of Payments statistics. While FDIs go exclusively to the private sector, a portion of portfolio and other investment flows finance governments as well (for example, Eurobonds issued by African governments are recorded as "portfolio flows," but the available data set does not allow the authors to remove them from the analysis).

Figure 13. Capital Inflows, by Income Group
(Billions of US dollars)

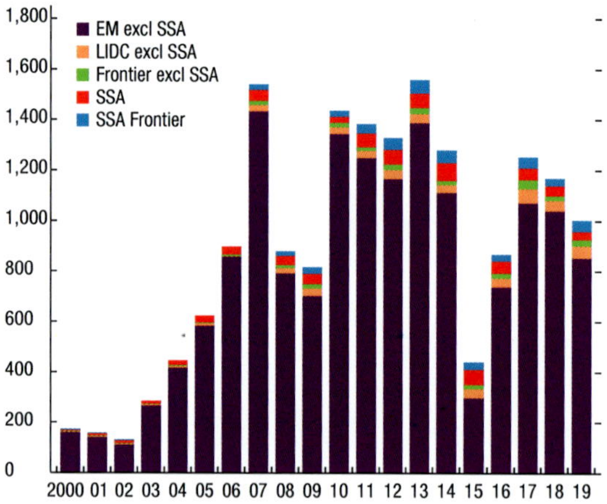

Sources: IMF *World Economic Outlook*; and IMF staff calculations.
Note: Inflows include foreign direct investment, portfolio investments, derivatives, and other. Capital inflows measured as net incurrence of liabilities includes both equity and debt liabilities. Outliers Mauritius and Luxembourg excluded.

Figure 14. Capital Inflows to Sub-Saharan Africa
(Billions of US dollars)

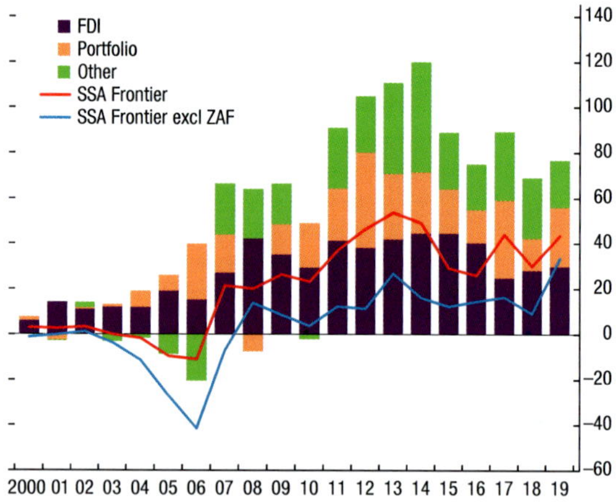

Sources: IMF *World Economic Outlook*; and IMF staff calculations.
Note: Inflows include foreign direct investment, portfolio investments, derivatives, and other. Capital inflows measured as net incurrence of liabilities includes both equity and debt liabilities. Outliers Mauritius and Luxembourg excluded.
FDI = foreign direct investment, ZAF = South Africa.

with a large proportion of all capital flows to SSA going toward large frontier markets, dominated by South Africa (Figure 14).

FDI inflows, a subset of private capital inflows representing longer-term investment into SSA, lag behind other developing regions. FDI is an important source of financing for economic development bringing with it not only capital but also employment and productivity improvements through management practices, skills transfer, innovation, and new technologies. To realize the economic potential of SSA and meet the growing development needs of the continent, more private finance through FDI is needed. SSA received FDI inflows equivalent to 0.7 of global GDP in 2018, compared with Asia (8.5 percent), Latin America (1.0 percent) and the Middle East and North Africa (0.3 percent) (Figure 15). FDI to SSA has remained relatively stable as a percent of aggregate SSA GDP over the last decade despite vulnerabilities from commodity price shocks in the region.

In addition, the scope for development driven by FDI is limited, as a large part of foreign investment coming to Africa is directed to extractive industries (UNCTAD 2019). To look at the sectoral allocation of investment, this paragraph uses a measure of "cross-border private investment," a subset of FDI that captures announced investment in new or the expansion of existing assets.[2] Figure 16 shows that investment into all SDG sectors[3] accounts for

[2]Data on cross-border investment are available from fDi Markets. https://www.fdimarkets.com/

[3]SDG sectors are defined using fDi Markets industry sector and subsector categories that best match SDG development sectors, education, health, roads, electricity, and water.

Figure 15. FDI Inflows, 2018
(Percent of global GDP)

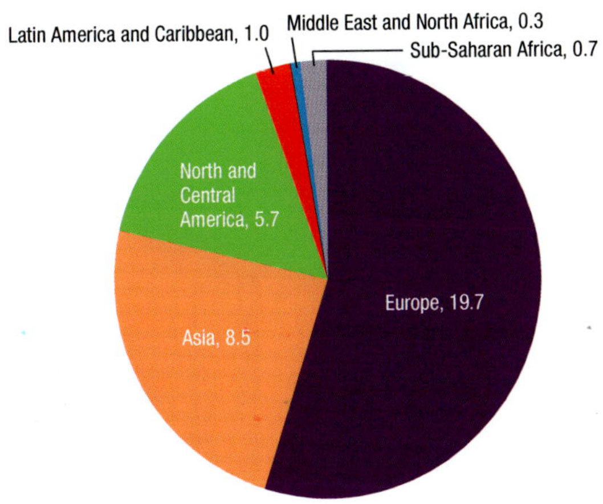

Source: IMF Coordinated Direct Investment Survey Database.
Note: FDI = foreign direct investment.

Figure 16. Cross Border Investment in SSA
(Millions of US dollars)

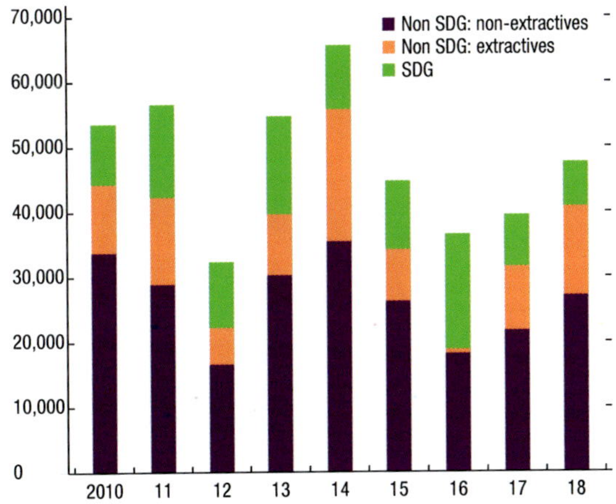

Sources: fDi Markets; and International Finance Corporation staff calculations.
Note: SDG = sustainable development goals.

about a quarter of cross-border investment in SSA during the period, with a broadly similar share of investment in extractives. SDG sector investment is dominated by the energy sector accounting for 82 percent, with investment in roads accounting for a further 13 percent, health sector investment 3 percent, and education and water and sanitation investment only 1 percent each (Figure 17).

Another way of looking at the extent of private finance in Africa is to examine the financing structure of infrastructure projects. The World Bank maintains a database of infrastructure investments with private participation (such as PPPs) across developing countries allowing for comparison over time. This type of investment has been volatile in SSA, with both the number of projects and the value invested falling in recent years (Figure 18). From a large spike in 2012, both in SSA ($15 billion) and across developing economies ($164 billion) there has been a fall in the number of projects and the values invested since then.

Who Invests in Africa in Development Sectors and How?

Bilateral and multilateral development institutions are generally the main international investors in infrastructure PPPs in Africa. The World Bank PPI database provides some information on the composition of financing for medium and large infrastructure projects with private participation. These figures should be treated with caution, since they are quite volatile from one year to the next, reflecting project-specific flows. During 2011–20, about 30 percent of total PPI investment in SSA countries was financed through

Figure 17. Cross Border Investment in SSA by SDG Sectors
(2009–18 cumulative)

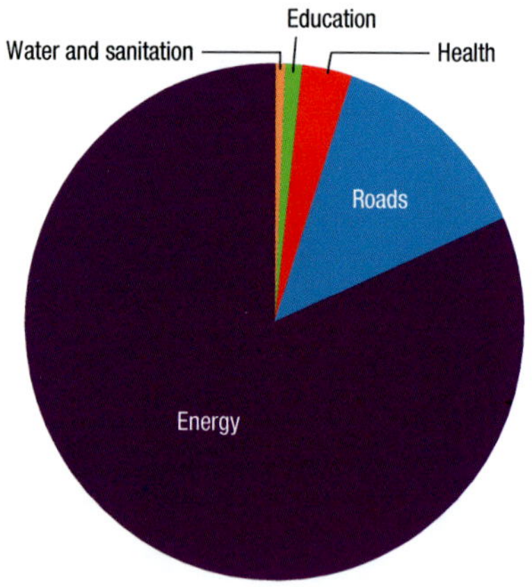

Sources: fDi Markets; and International Finance Corporation staff calculations.
Note: SDG = sustainable development goals.

Figure 18. Investment in Infrastructure with Private Participation in SSA, 2009–19

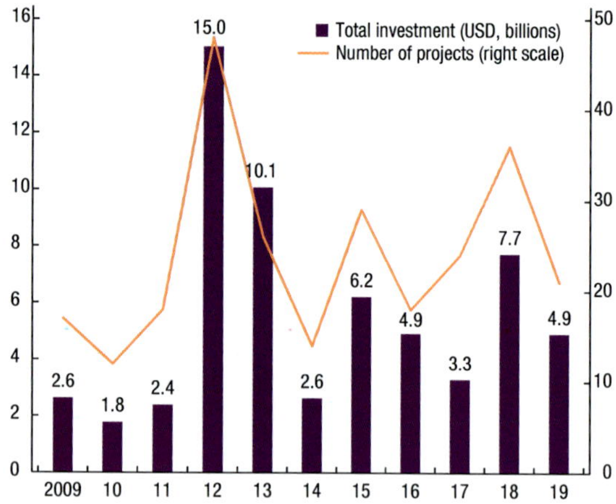

Source: Private Participation in Infrastructure Projects Database, World Bank.

international debt provided by bilateral and multiateral development finance institutions (DFIs), as illustrated by Figure 19.[4] On average, the contribution of international banks was relatively small over the period, although banks can be key investors in certain projects and/or in particular years.[5]

In addition, international investors typically use "funds" to finance projects. Private financial investors (either individuals or collective investment vehicles) can take equity stakes in listed African companies or provide debt financing through bonds. However, these direct forms of investment may not be available or easily accessible for all development sectors (for example, health or education) and are constrained by the shallowness of financial markets in Africa. Therefore, instead of investing directly, international investors use generally a two-tier structure to finance non-listed domestic companies and projects (Figure 20). The funds are specialized in what is called "alternative investments," investments outside the traditional assets. This is because many development projects rely on assets that have an unconventional and illiquid nature and require specific financing schemes such as special purpose vehicles. Typically, the funds are owned by and receive money from limited partnerships (LPs) and are managed by general partnerships (GPs). A fund will invest the LPs' financing in multiple investments, companies or projects,

[4]DFIs are public institutions owned by national governments or international development agencies that invest in private sector projects with a social or developmental focus.

[5]In the PPI database, "commercial debt" is the debt raised from commercial banks, not necessarily all debt raised on commercial terms. In Figure 19 the financing provided by international banks, which corresponds to international debt excluding DFIs and governments, represents about 6 percent of total investment over the period.

Figure 19. Sources of Financing for PPI Infrastructure Projects in SSA Countries, 2011–20
(Share of total investment)

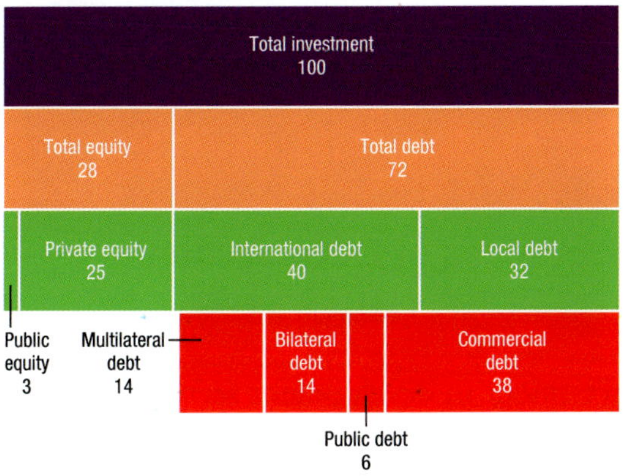

Source: World Bank Private Participation in Infrastructure database.

Figure 20. Investor Structure

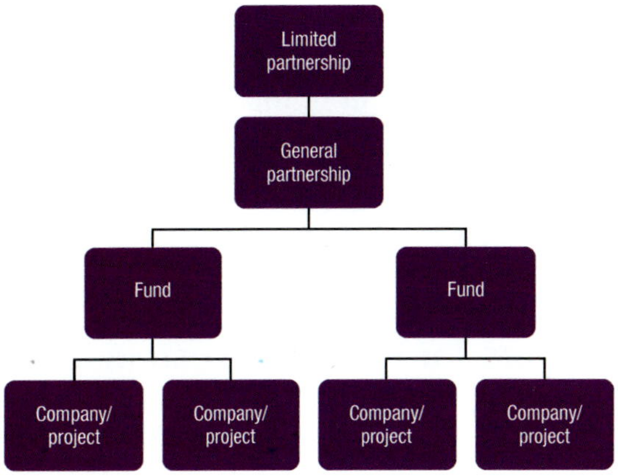

Source: IMF staff.

through which the fund makes a return that is paid back to the LP. Funds can be classified according to their main (alternative) asset class, such as private equity, private debt, infrastructure, or natural resources.

Across existing investment fund types, private equity funds are the main vehicle for investing in Africa. Global investment in development sectors is typically through funds dedicated to private equity, private debt, and infrastructure/real assets.[6] But, in Africa, private equity funds seem predominant (McKinsey 2020). From 2010 to 2017, survey results on Africa-focused funds show private equity funds have invested $9.3 billion in managed assets; infrastructure funds have invested $6.1 billion; and private debt/credit funds have invested close to $1 billion (EMPEA 2018).[7] The main investors in the private equity asset class in Africa are DFIs (30 percent of all assets under management in private equity funds), pension funds (25 percent), along with third-party fund managers (15 percent), while direct investors, foundations, and asset managers make up the remainder (AVCA 2019).

Alternative forms of investment designed to fit the unique needs of investors in development sectors are gradually becoming mainstream in SSA. "Impact investment" is a growing form of investment in SSA, through various assets classes (for example, equity or debt), that does not solely target financial

[6]There is some overlap among categories, since infrastructure funds rely on debt and equity finance, while private equity funds and private debt funds can also invest in infrastructure projects (although this is not their main focus).

[7]Assets raised by GPs from LP investors can be greater than the funds actually invested; GPs hold this unspent capital or "dry powder" while in search of bankable projects.

returns but are made with the intention to generate positive, measurable social and environmental impact (Box 2).[8] Impact investment is becoming an important source of financing in SSA. The region received 11 percent of total impact investors assets under management (AUM) in 2019 ($221 billion globally, based on a sample of 289 impact-investing organizations) (GIIN 2020).

What Factors Explain the Lack of Attractiveness of Development Sectors for Foreign Investors in Africa?

The low contribution of private investment in development sectors in SSA is an indication that the perceived risk-return profile is often not attractive enough. Both anecdotally and empirical work show that returns in Africa were high in the 2000s compared to other developing regions but have declined significantly in the past decade. At the same time, risks that deter financial investors—such as institutional settings, size and liquidity of markets, and macroeconomic volatility—are higher in SSA and have not declined markedly over the same period. The analysis below echoes the findings of other recent papers. For instance, focusing on the group of institutional investors, Juvonen and others (2019) find that the average return on investment over a 10-year period was not higher in Africa than in developed markets, while risks were perceived to be more elevated.

Returns

This analysis focuses on two types of returns in development sectors in SSA: those at the investment fund level and those at the company/project level. The analysis is based on "private returns"—which are those that are relevant for investors—and disregards the "social returns," which are likely to be quite high in Africa and significantly above private returns (Collier 2014).

- *Financial returns* (also called fund-level returns) are defined as the returns recorded at the fund level and captured by the financial investors.[9]
- *Project returns* (also called firm-level returns) are defined as the returns generated by a company/project and measured as the profit generated divided by the assets or equity of the project (return on assets ROA or return on equity ROE).[10]

[8]This is the Global Impact Investment Network's definition.
[9]Given data constraints, the analysis is limited to private equity funds and venture capital.
[10]Firm and company are used interchangeably in this section.

Table 1. Private Equity and Venture Capital Fund Returns
(Horizon Pooled Returns in US dollar terms, Net to Limited Partners as of December 31, 2019)

	1-Year	3-Year	5-Year	10-Year	15-Year	20-Year
Africa Private Equity and Venture Capital Index	4.7	5.8	2.7	4.9	6.0	6.6
US Private Equity Index	18.6	16.8	14.2	15.9	13.3	11.4
Cambridge Associates LLC US Venture Capital Index	19.3	16.2	12.1	14.6	11.0	6.6
MSCI Emerging Markets Index	18.9	12.0	6.0	4.0	7.9	7.0
MSCI World Index	27.7	12.6	8.7	9.5	6.9	4.5
S&P 500 Index	31.5	15.3	11.7	13.6	9.0	6.1

Source: Cambridge Associates (2020b, c, d).
Notes: The Index is a horizon calculation based on data compiled from 693 emerging markets private equity and venture capital funds, including fully liquidated partnerships, formed between 1986 and 2019. Pooled horizon internal rate of return (IIR) calculations, net of fees, expenses and carried interest.

Constraints on data availability warrant the use of multiple return metrics. While *financial returns* of the funds are best for the analysis (since they are a key consideration for financial investors), only *project returns* are available at the sectoral level. In addition, financial returns are available only for a subset of funds and data are rarely disclosed. As a result, this chapter uses both sources to analyze returns.

On average, *financial returns* in Africa seem to have underperformed comparable benchmarks in the past two decades. Given data constraints, the analysis focuses on private equity and venture capital funds, for which comparable return data are available across regions. Cambridge Associates (2020b, c, d) shows that average returns (using internal rate of returns) generated by Africa-focused private equity and venture capital funds tend to lag behind US private equity performance indicators as well as MSCI indexes (Table 1). Over the past 15 years, for instance, the returns of the Africa index averaged 6.0 percent a year, compared to 13.3 percent for the US private equity index and 7.9 percent for the MSCI Emerging Markets Index.

Nonetheless, Africa's financial returns were higher in the 2000s and early 2010s. When analyzing the returns of Africa-focused private equity and venture capital funds over time, an interesting pattern emerges: returns for African "liquidated funds" (that is, at the time of exit) were higher than in other regions of the world, while "active funds" (still open) have much lower expected returns, indicating lower expected cashflows throughout the investment (Figure 21; IFC 2018b). This difference between liquidated and active fund returns may be due to the commodity price collapse of 2014 and related currency depreciations, which have lowered the realized and expected returns in US dollars of active funds, while liquidated funds correspond to a period of economic boom in Africa (from the mid-2000s to the early 2010s).[11] In fact, Africa-focused private equity funds outperformed

[11]Another possible explanation for the discrepancy between returns across types of funds is that underperforming projects are kept in open funds. Indeed, it takes longer to close and exit funds that include "lame ducks."

Figure 21. Private Equity and Venture Capital Investment Returns by Region, as of 2017
(Net internal rate of return, percent)

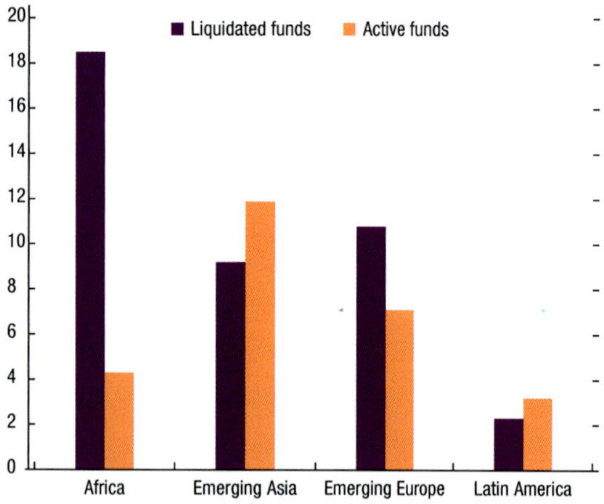

Sources: Cambridge Associates; and IFC (2018b).
Note: "Cambridge Associates LLC Private Investments Database; AVCA Focus Series 2018 Private Benchmarks for Africa." The database includes 24 participating fund managers, 51 institutional quality Africa-focused private equity and venture capital funds, and more than 450 unique portfolio investments in nearly 400 companies. Vintage year coverage: 1995 to 2015; total fund capitalization: US$12.6 billion of commitments; average fund size: US$248 million, ranging from <US$50 million to >US$800 million. Geographic strategies of funds: South African (13 funds), pan-African (34 funds), other regional (four funds). Individual investments headquartered in 33 different African countries.

US venture capital and emerging market benchmarks in the 2000s decade (AVCA 2013). In addition to the commodity price shock, Mittal (2020) also suggests other explanations for the relatively low returns of private equity in Africa, including more conservative investment strategies, a low number of attractive projects (which creates competition), and some characteristics of the transactions. Difficulties to exit due to low liquidity also hurt investment returns in Africa (PEI 2020).

Regarding *project returns* in SSA, they have been high in the past, but have fallen since the end of the 2000s and are now similar to comparator developing regions. Firm-level data from Bureau van Dijk databases are used to assess financial returns annually of firms operating domestically but with foreign capital (see Annex 3 for method and definitions). Comparisons cover both annual ROE and ROA. In SSA, the period 2000–07 saw high ROEs, exceeding on average 20 percent, well above other developing regions. But for 2008–17, following the 2008 global financial crisis and the commodity prices shock of 2014, returns in SSA dropped dramatically to below 15 percent, on average, reaching levels comparable to other developing regions (Figures 22 and 23).

Project returns, measured as spreads, paint a similar story. Table 2 presents the project return spreads (also called "risk-adjusted returns"), by region, using firm-level data indicating the premium return made above domestic sovereign benchmark rates.[12] Spreads based on ROE have fallen significantly after a peak in 2006–07, and have, in most recent years, gotten closer to spreads observed in other regions..

Project returns also vary across different sectors of the economy. Some evidence suggests that overall returns tend to be somewhat lower in SDG-related

[12]The "risk-adjusted returns" are defined as returns removing the risk-free rates (government 1-year T-bill or bond rates, subject to data availability by country).

Figure 22. Return on Equity
(Median, percent)

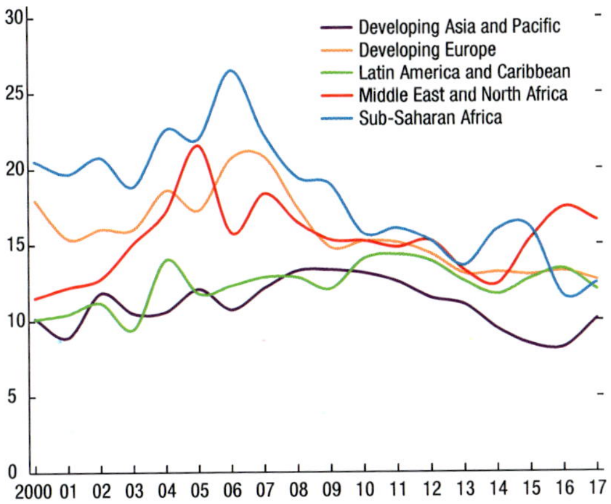

Sources: Orbis Van Djik Database; and IMF staff calculations.
Note: Observations = developing Asia and Pacific 2,465, developing Europe 6,668, Latin America and Caribbean 274, Middle East and North America 122, sub-Saharan Africa 41.

Figure 23. Return on Assets
(Median, percent)

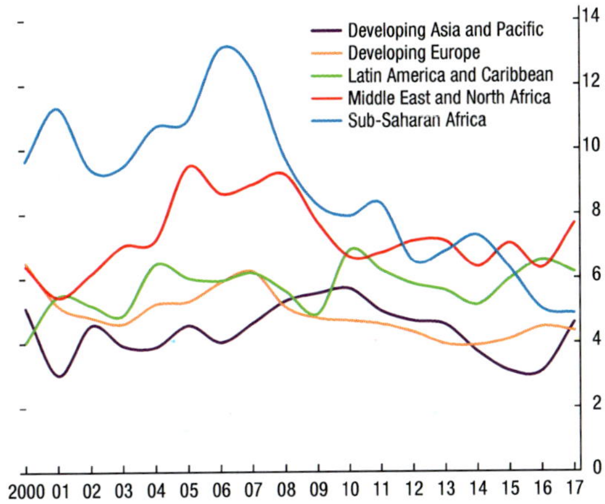

Sources: Orbis Van Djik Database; and IMF staff calculations.
Note: Observations = developing Asia and Pacific 2,465, developing Europe 6,668, Latin America and Caribbean 274, Middle East and North America 122, sub-Saharan Africa 41.

Table 2. Firms' Return on Equity Spreads by Region
(Percent)

	Annual medians 2000–2007			
	2000	2003	2006	2007
Developing Asia and Pacific	5.9	8.2	6.5	9.7
Developing Europe	9.7	10.6	13.6	14.0
Latin America and Caribbean	−3.7	3.6	5.2	4.7
Middle East and North Africa	4.5	7.4	11.1	13.3
Sub-Saharan Africa	9.2	9.2	18.8	14.0
	Annual medians 2008–2017			
	2008	2011	2014	2017
Developing Asia and Pacific	10.9	9.5	7.8	8.5
Developing Europe	10.1	7.7	5.7	5.8
Latin America and Caribbean	4.4	9.0	5.3	4.0
Middle East and North Africa	10.6	9.3	8.1	2.6
Sub-Saharan Africa	11.5	11.4	8.8	4.8

Source: Bureau Van Dijk; and IMF staff calculations.
Note: Spreads' median is computed across firms for a given year.

sectors compared to non-SDG sectors at the global level.[13] For instance, developing Asia-Pacific and Latin America and the Caribbean both have lower median ROE, while, in developing Europe and Middle East and North Africa, the ROE in SDG and non-SDG sectors are broadly similar. Interestingly, this does not appear to be the case in SSA, where several SDG

[13]SDG sectors are defined using standard NACE Revision 2 standard-sector categories that best match SDG development sectors, education, health, roads, electricity, and water.

Table 3. Return on Equity of Firms, by Region and Sector, 2000–2017
(Median, Percent)

	Developing Asia and Pacific	Developing Europe	Latin America and Caribbean	Middle East and North Africa	Sub-Saharan Africa
Non-SDG Sectors	11.2	15.0	12.5	14.9	17.7
Agriculture	11.8	11.6	8.7	6.2	12.0
Mining	18.0	17.3	16.4	30.3	21.6
Manufacturing	11.7	13.6	12.2	15.2	18.3
Services	9.0	16.2	13.1	12.9	17.6
SDG Sectors	6.9	15.2	11.0	15.3	20.7
SDG-Education	12.5	13.6	7.3	13.0	19.6
SDG-Electricity	8.0	12.7	11.1	29.5	27.0
SDG-Health	9.1	20.9	...	7.4	...
SDG-Infrastructure	7.5	16.1	11.2	19.4	37.0
SDG-Water	4.8	11.8	6.8	19.2	19.3

Source: Bureau Van Dijk; and IMF staff calculations.
Note: There are no observations recorded in the SDG health sector for SSA and LAC in the sample defined in Annex 3.

sectors in SSA command high returns including infrastructure and electricity (although this result should be interpreted with caution due to the small sample size of projects in SSA, as indicated in Annex 3). When comparing sectors across developing regions, infrastructure projects have had a median return on equity of 37 percent in SSA, well above the next highest Middle East and North Africa (19.4 percent) or developing Europe (16.1 percent) (Table 3). Similarly, electricity investment projects in SSA received a high return of 27 percent, second only to Middle East and North Africa.

Risks

International investors report risks to be relatively high in SSA. A GIIN survey of impact investors show 24 percent of investors in SSA experienced a "significant risk"[14] event in the region in 2017, second only to Latin America with 31 percent of respondents. South Asia by comparison reported only 15 percent of respondents (GIIN 2018).

The ongoing COVID-19 pandemic has already affected international investors' perceived risk. A recent survey shows globally 81 percent of impact investors perceived overall investment risk as likely or very likely to have changed as result of the pandemic due to macroeconomic, liquidity, and currency risks (GIIN 2020). Despite this elevated risk assessment, 15 percent of investors are likely to commit more capital in development sectors of low-income countries and emerging market economies in response to the pandemic.

[14]The 2018 GIIN survey reports "significant risk events" experienced by respondents during 2017. That year, these risks included complex and changing economic and political environments, corruption, and extreme weather events.

Figure 24. Contributors of Risk to Impact Investment Portfolios
(Percent of global respondents indicating severe risk)

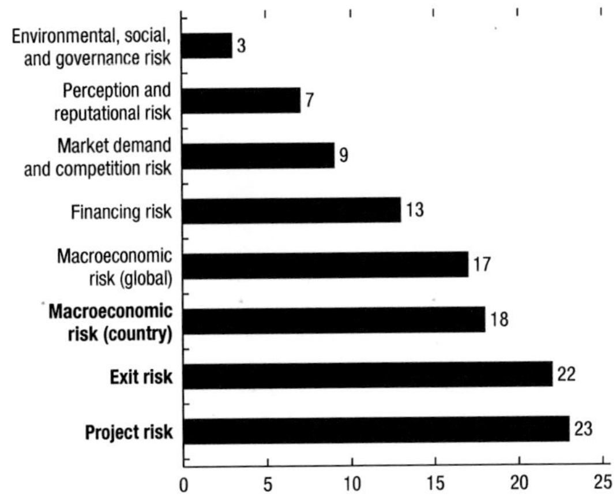

Source: Annual Impact Investor Survey 2020, Global Impact Investing Network.

Assessing the risk of investing in SSA includes both uncertainties about generating returns on the ground and the ability of foreign investors to recoup returns out of country. According to global institutional investors and fund managers, there is no standard source of information on risk and macroeconomic uncertainties used when making investment decisions. Instead a series of benchmarks, indices, and firsthand experiences on the ground are used to inform decision making. Figure 24 summarizes the main risks identified by impact investors investing across different regions in the world (including Africa), as a proxy for investor views in development sectors. Three key risks are identified by impact investors: (1) *project risk* wherein projects are not "investment-ready" or "bankable"; (2) *macroeconomic risk* wherein economic or political uncertainty limits the ability to generate money from the investment; and (3) *exit risk,* which is the ability to monetize the investment at the desired time and repatriate the funds. Studies focusing on Africa (Juvonen and others 2019, AVCA 2020a) as well as interviews conducted in the context of this paper with a large number of financial investors highlight similar risks and bottlenecks.

Project Risk

The ability to identify bankable projects and manage the execution of projects is a key constraint identified by international investors. Project risk covers both the risks of poor selection and poor execution of the project and how likely they are to get to completion and, ultimately, yield returns. Identifying "bankable" projects is a key stumbling block in SSA for several reasons. There is a lack of well-advanced proposals that can attract international investors. Capacity constraints and preparation costs limit the pipeline of investment-ready projects that require proof of project feasibility, financial viability, and regulatory and legal compliance. Information gaps to identify, assess, and monitor projects, along with misperceptions of risk in SSA, also limit the appetite for investment.

Figure 25. Cancelled or Distressed PPP Investment, 1983–2020
(Percent)

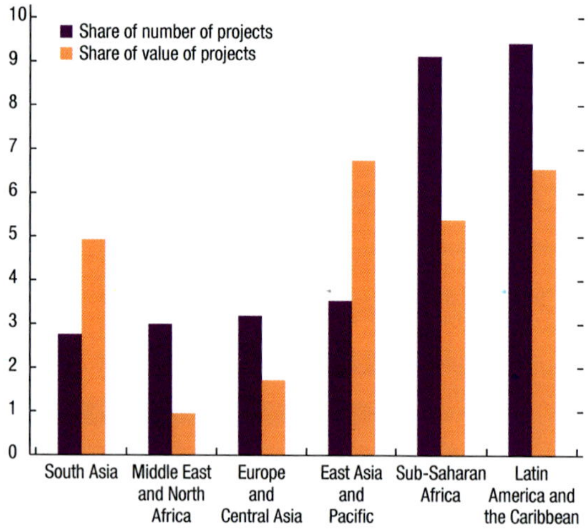

Sources: Private Participation in Investment Database, World Bank; and IMF staff calculations.

Figure 26. Project Finance Default Rates, 1983–2018
(Percent, based on Basel definition of default)

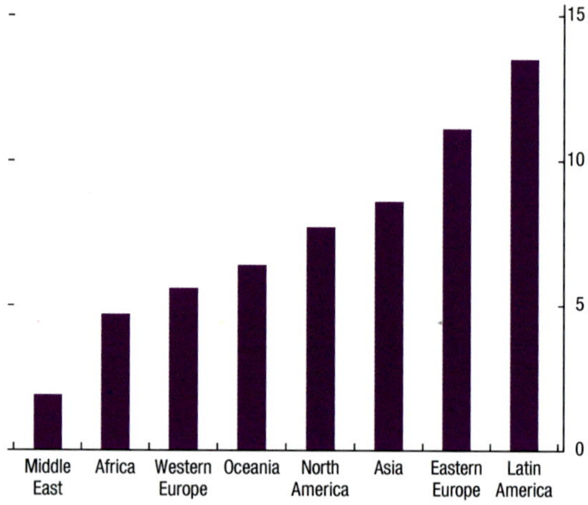

Source: Moody's Investors Service (2020a), Default and Recovery Rates for Project Finance Bank Loans.

Assessing project risk is, in essence, a microeconomic exercise. But, some macroeconomic indicators give a sense of the extent of project risk in Africa. Figures 25 and 26 show an interesting picture: a large volume of projects does not come to fruition in SSA, although, when they do, default rates seem to be lower. Indeed, SSA has a high rate of project failure in infrastructure compared to most developing regions except Latin America, as illustrated by the proportion of cancelled or distressed PPP investments, either expressed as a share of total projects' investment or number of projects (Figure 25). However, infrastructure projects seem to display lower default rates, according to Moody's project finance database, which records unrated project finance bank loans. Although default history is limited in Africa and results should be treated with caution, Moody's Investors Service (2020a) estimates the simple average default rate during 1983–2018 (measured as the count of defaults divided by the count of projects) at 4.7 percent in Africa compared to a global average of 6.8 percent (Figure 26). Cumulative default rates for cohorts starting in 1990 also place Africa below most other regions.[15]

[15]Moody's has also a separate data set on rated infrastructure debt, showing that the five-year cumulative default rate are relatively high (10 percent) for these securities in developing countries and ratings are lower (Ba1/Ba2), but the sample size is very small and no separate information is available for Africa (Moody's Investors Service 2020b).

Figure 27. Exchange Rate Movements Against USD by Region, 2010–19
(Standard deviation (left scale), index 2010 = 100 (right scale))

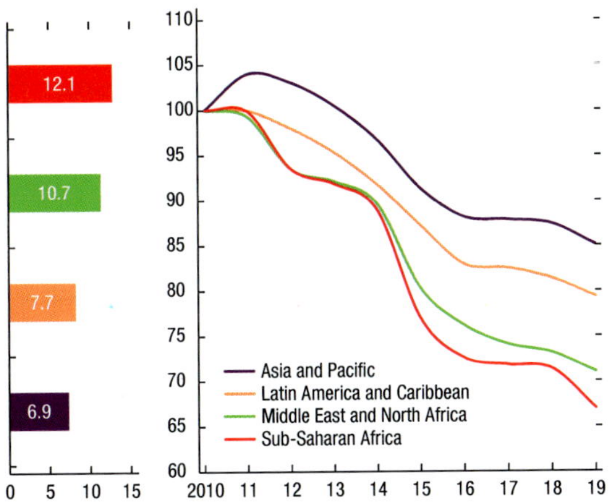

Source: IMF *World Economic Outlook*; and IMF staff estimates.

Figure 28. Real GDP Growth by Region, 2010–19
(Standard deviation (left scale), percent (right scale))

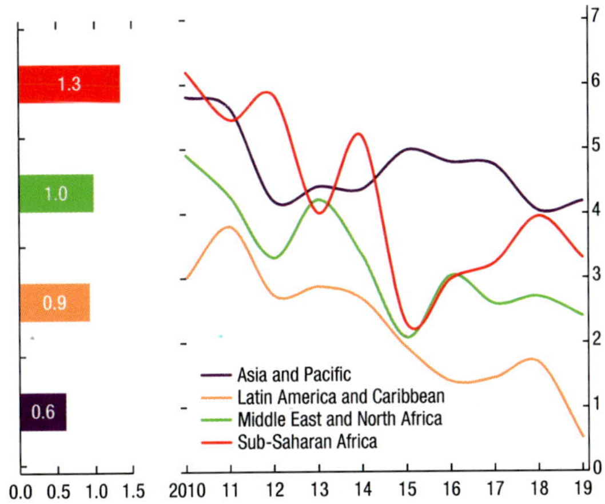

Sources: IMF *World Economic Outlook*; and IMF staff estimates.

Macroeconomic Risk

Uncertainties on key economic variables create a challenging environment for international investors. Macroeconomic risk has many dimensions, but one type of risk that investors are particularly concerned about is an unanticipated currency depreciation. When returns are actualized and remitted to the investors, very little could remain of the margin due to large unforeseen deprecations. Currency risk is apparent when looking into the depreciation against the US dollar and comparing SSA against other emerging regions, wherein SSA compares poorly. This implies that an investor's return for a project denominated in local currency (with the average holding time of a private financing project in SSA of about 5–8 years) can potentially lose a third of this due to the depreciation or will have had large hedging costs to secure against the downward pressure of the local currency (Figure 27).

GDP growth volatility also limits revenues growth and, therefore, returns in SSA. Shocks to growth can affect financial viability. GDP growth in SSA is particularly volatile compared to other developing countries (Figure 28). This is as result of a wide range of factors: (1) heavy reliance on commodities; (2) small size of automatic stabilizers in governments' budgets; (3) political instability and poor governance; (4) economic structures that are reliant on agriculture (and dependent on weather); and (5) inadequate health infrastructure, which make countries more vulnerable to health shocks.

Assessing macroeconomic risk through sovereign risk ratings in SSA is difficult as they are generally poor or nonexistent. Sovereign ratings provide

Figure 29. Moody's Sovereign Credit Ratings
(Latest available)

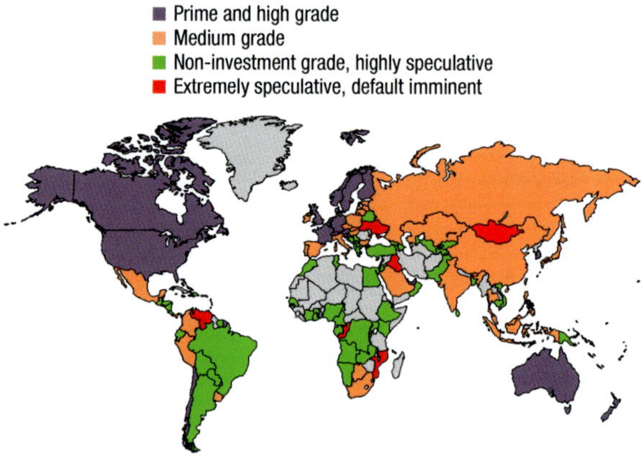

Source: Moody's Investors Service.

a complementary and independent assessment for a financial investor to evaluate a country's macroeconomic risk. Investors will typically use sovereign rating as the baseline for their risk assessment. However, Figure 29 shows SSA ratings are generally poor, either non-investment grade or speculative, if there is a rating at all (gray in the map indicates no rating available). Where there is no sovereign rating, it is more difficult for investors to calibrate their risk premiums.

Exit Risk[16]

Investment exit seems to be more difficult in SSA than in other regions. Exiting an investment is critical for investors' ability to create value across their portfolios. The number of exits from African private equity funds is small (although reflecting the relatively small size of Africa in the world economy) and the average holding period for firms has been increasing, indicating difficulties to exit at the right price (Figure 30). In a survey by the African Private Equity and Venture Capital Association published in March 2020, 76 percent of LPs identified limited exit opportunities as a key challenge for GPs in the African continent over the next three years (AVCA 2020a). The situation seems to have worsened; 65 percent held this view in the 2018 survey, and 58 percent in 2017. Relatedly, 42 percent of LPs view the relatively long holding periods for portfolio companies as the biggest challenge for investing in African private equity. These difficulties to exit are mostly due to three main bottlenecks in SSA: (1) relatively underdeveloped and illiquid financial markets, which make it complicated to sell assets; (2) weaknesses of the judicial, policy, and regulatory frameworks, which also constrain or impede the ability to sell (due to bureaucratic and legal hurdles) or the ability to recoup gains (due to expropriation or confiscation of private returns by the state); and (3) capital account restrictions on financial outflows. The following paragraphs further examine these three bottlenecks.

[16]Exit occurs when investors sell their stake in a firm or investment. Exit risk is the risk for investors to successfully realize and, if applicable, repatriate their expected returns within a planned time frame.

Figure 30. Private Equity Exit Activity in Africa, 2007–18

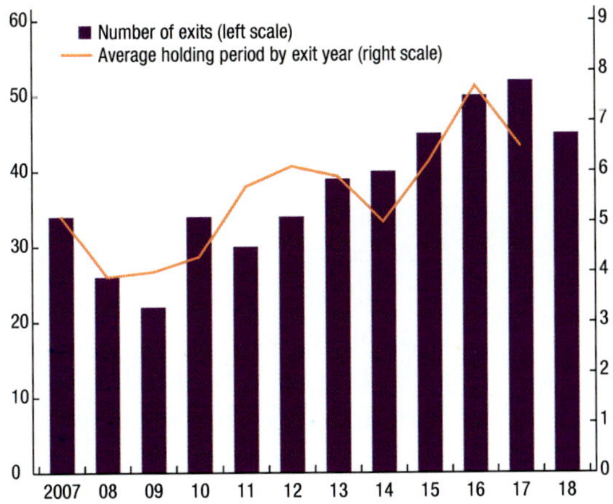

Sources: E&Y and AVCA (2018); and AVCA (2020b).

Figure 31. Index of Financial Development, 2008–18
(Percent)

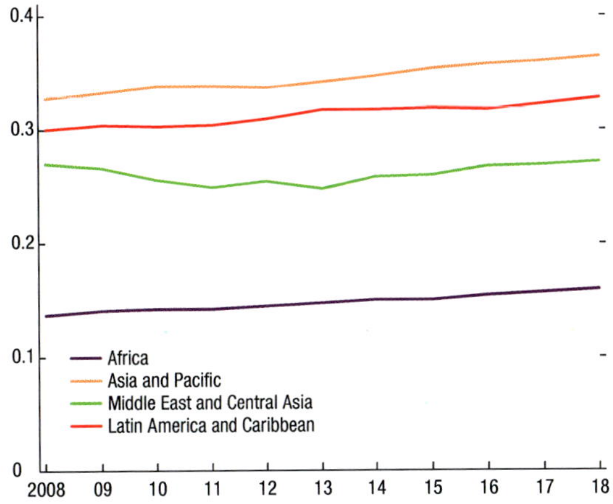

Sources: IMF Financial Development Index; Sahay and others (2015).

Domestic financial markets, including stock exchanges, are small and underdeveloped in SSA. They are dominated by the South Africa Johannesburg Stock Exchange that accounts for more than 90 percent of total market capitalization.[17] Liquidity is low, and small trading sizes are common, far smaller than many funds' minimum trading size, which is a limiting constraint for many investors looking for alternative markets to invest (Figure 31). For this reason, as shown in Figure 32, many private equity exits in Africa are through management buy-outs (MBOs), private sales or to trade buyers (trade sale) rather than initial public offerings (IPO) or sales to financial buyers including other private equity funds, who are the typical buyers in other more developed financial markets (EY & AVCA 2018).

Figure 32. Private Equity Exit Routes in Africa, 2007–17
(Percent)

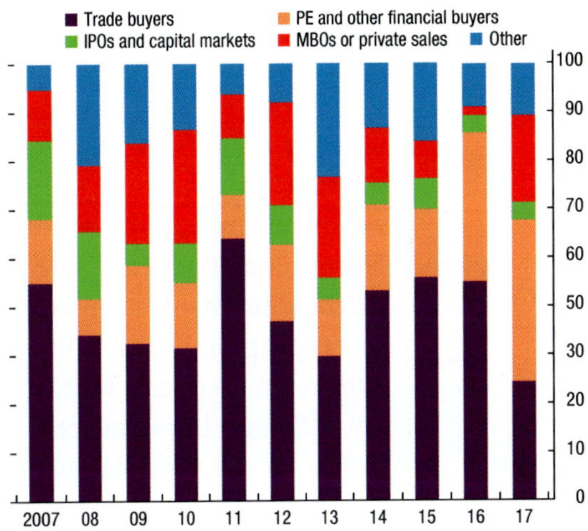

Source: E&Y and AVCA (2018).
Note: IPO = initial public offering; MBO = management buyout; PE = private equity.

[17]World Federation of Exchanges database, reported in the World Bank World Development Indicators.

Figure 33. Selected Indicators of Investor Protection, 2019
(Index 1–7 where 7 is best; median scores across regional country groups)

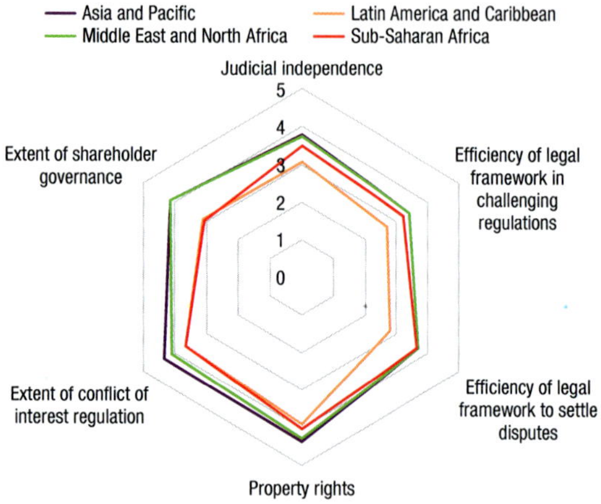

Source: World Economic Forum, *Global Competivness Report 2019.*

Failure to enforce legal and regulatory rights of shareholders can also compound the risk of exiting. Despite some improvements over the years, the regulatory and legal system is often challenging to navigate. SSA records relatively low scores for indicators that measure the legal protection of investors, according to WEF (2019).[18] In particular, SSA has the lowest median scores among all regions for shareholder governance and conflict of interest regulation (Figure 33).[19] Nonetheless, many African countries fare better than those in Latin American across other legal and judicial indicators. Overall, the enforcement of the rule of law and regulations is often uneven and unpredictable in SSA, which is compounded by the weak capacity of lawmakers and some country officials. A shortage of well-trained lawyers, accountants, and other professionals can slow the necessary process for regular business transactions, as well as impede the resolution of legal issues through courts (IFC 2018b). More generally, weak governance and corruption in the public sector can discourage financial investors, because these elements represent a threat to the appropriability of their profits. Businesses do not get started, thrive, and expand in countries that do not provide sound regulation, market-supporting laws that are implemented fairly and consistently by honest and well-trained judges, and a transparent procurement system. Both the 2020 Transparency International Corruption Index and the 2020 Worldwide Governance Indicator on "control of corruption" show that SSA countries score and rank, on average, below other regions when it comes to the perception of corruption.

Finally, capital outflow restrictions, which are widespread in SSA countries, may complicate divesture operations for foreign entities. African countries

[18]International competitiveness and doing business indicators should be interpreted with caution because they are based on surveys of perceptions by enterprises, citizens, and experts and their methodology generates margins of error for each governance estimate. Estimates reflect the relative, not the absolute, performance of the country.

[19]"Conflict of interest regulation" measures the protection of shareholders against directors' misuse of corporate assets for personal gain. "Shareholder governance" measures the shareholders' rights in corporate governance, including corporate decisions making, safeguards, and transparency.

have gradually liberalized their capital accounts since the 1980s. Jahan and Wang (2016) find a relatively high level of capital account openness for nonresidents in SSA countries, but the openness on outflows remains very limited (Figure 34). In 2013 (last year reviewed by the authors), 11 SSA countries maintained full control on purchase and sale transactions by nonresidents, and 14 countries had full control on outflows, with openness indices equal to zero in these countries on a scale from 0 to 1. In addition, Gupta and Masetti (2018) show that restrictions on nonresident outflows in SSA have not eased as rapidly as in other regions during the past decade.

Figure 34. Indices of Capital Account Openness in Developing Regions
(Median, 2013)

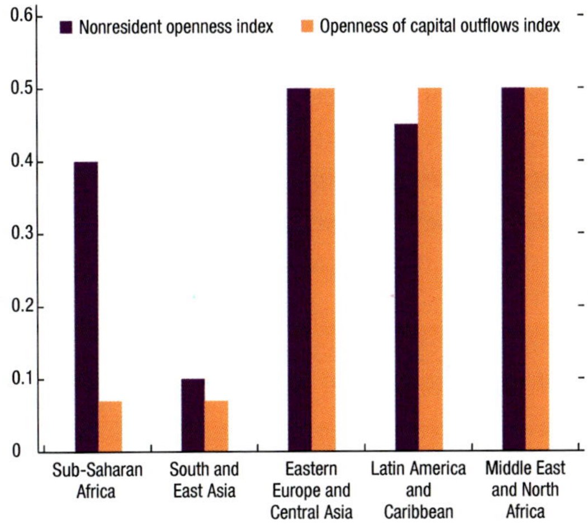

Source: Jahan and Wang (2016).
Note: Indices range between 0 and 1. Higher index value means greater openness.

Box 2. Impact Investors in SSA

Impact investment is an emerging approach to investment that sits along a spectrum between philanthropy and traditional investment that seek only financial returns. Impact Investment provides an opportunity to use the private investment into SSA towards development sectors addressing social or environmental needs (UNDP 2016). There is a range of impact investors: some target market rate financial returns while others target below-market returns either as not-for-profit funds or alternative nonfinancial metrics (including social and environmental). In a recent survey of impact investors at the global level, more than 80 percent of respondents indicated progress toward the SDG agenda as a "very" or "somewhat" important motivation to their fund goals providing a framework for investment priorities (GIIN 2020).

Box Figure 2.1. Impact Investing Asset Allocations by Region
(Total fund assets US$ 221 billion)

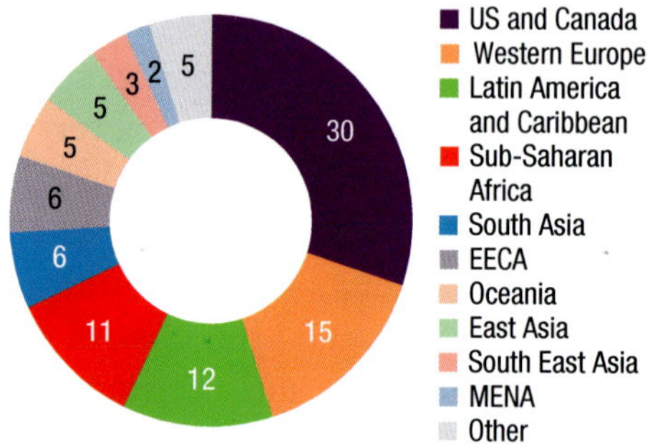

Source: Global Impact Investor Survey, 2020.
Note: Percent of assets under management excluding outliers. "Other" denotes assets allocated globally. EECA = Eastern Europe and Central Asia; MENA = Middle East and North Africa.

GIIN (2020) report shows 11 percent of assets are allocated to SSA, fourth behind North America, western Europe, and Latin America and the Caribbean (Box Figure 2.1). Other surveys, based on a smaller number of investors, find an even larger share for SSA (see, for instance, Cambridge Associates 2020a). However, globally only a small fraction of the impact investment assets is allocated to education (3 percent), infrastructure (4 percent), healthcare (7 percent), and water sanitation and hygiene (6 percent). By contrast, energy receives 16 percent of impact-investing assets currently. Most of the funds go also to financial services and microfinance, food and agriculture, and forestry.

Chapter

4 Creating a Business Environment More Conducive to Private Finance

This chapter describes policies meant to improve the business environment and remove government-induced barriers that discourage private ventures in Africa. A targeted strategy focused on mitigating three main risks perceived by international investors (project risk, macroeconomic risk, and exit risk) is likely to be superior to a more diluted and piecemeal approach that implements a generic list of private sector development reforms. In addition to horizontal (economywide) policies, the chapter also highlights the need for tailored sector-specific reforms.

Horizontal Policies: Mitigating Three Economywide Risks

The purpose of horizontal policies is to alleviate the main risks perceived by international investors at the country level. As shown in Chapter 3, investments in developing economies are particularly exposed to three main risks, which rank at the top of investors' sentiment surveys: project risk, macroeconomic risk, and exit risk. Countries willing to attract international investors in development sectors should tackle these bottlenecks as a priority. The best course of action, especially for countries with limited capacity, is to focus their efforts on a few key barriers rather than trying to fix the whole business environment in a diluted and potentially inconsistent manner (Hausmann, Rodrik, and Velasco 2006).

Addressing Project Risk

To attract financial investors, projects need to be "bankable." A project is considered "bankable" or "investment-ready" when it is financially viable, sufficiently developed and mature, and has a relatively large size (Oberholzer and others 2018). Like in other regions of the world, international investors in Africa finance primarily enterprises and projects that have proven business models, and available and reliable data to assess their performance (UNDP 2015). In practice, factors required to demonstrate bankability include proof of project feasibility, sufficient development, financial viability, demand planning, sound funding of operations, acceptance in the community, regulatory approvals, and legal compliance. Nonetheless, even projects that do not generate adequate cash flows can be "bankable" provided that various risk mitigations or credit enhancements are available (IFC 2018b).

In SSA, the pipeline of well-structured and investment-ready projects is relatively limited in the eyes of international investors. Although many argue that private capital is not scarce worldwide, a common complaint of investors is the insufficient pipeline of projects in developing countries and, more specifically in Africa (Kortekaas 2015, Mercer LLC 2018, Tyson 2018). A majority of African PPP-announced projects are not realized because they proved to be either poorly designed or not commercially viable (Maury and de Féligonde 2019). Relatedly, there is a high degree of competition for quality assets among investors in Africa (Deloitte 2019).

Several impediments tend to constrain projects' bankability in Africa. These impediments mainly concern capacity constraints, cost considerations, project size, and information gaps:

- *Capacity constraints to generate deals.* Governments, local institutions, and project managers lack the technical capability to bring projects to the market in a manner that will satisfy potential bidders and to prepare projects to the standards required by private sponsors and financial investors (IFC 2018b). The lack of capacity to generate, manage, and assess projects is seen as a key barrier for infrastructure provision in developing countries (IMF 2016a).
- *Cost of project preparation.* Partly due to these capacity constraints, project preparation costs can be significant and constrain the bankability of projects. Depending on the sector, they can be as high as 4–10 percent of the total investment for infrastructure projects in Africa (Mayaki 2019). As a result, projects are often abandoned at an early stage of the project preparation phase.
- *Size requirements.* Figure 35 shows that, while international private equity investors typically invest in projects larger than $100 million, more than 70 percent of companies are situated in the range of $25 million and below in SSA countries (Schlapinski 2018).[1] Only 10 percent of international private equity funds target these relatively smaller-size companies below

[1]Looking at the broader sample of institutional investors, Juvonen and others (2019) find that the minimum deal size for smaller-size institutional investors is $100 million, while large global institutional investors are interested in minimum-ticket size of more than $500 million.

Figure 35. Private Companies by Revenue in Selected Sub-Saharan African Countries
(Percent of companies in sample; 2014–17)

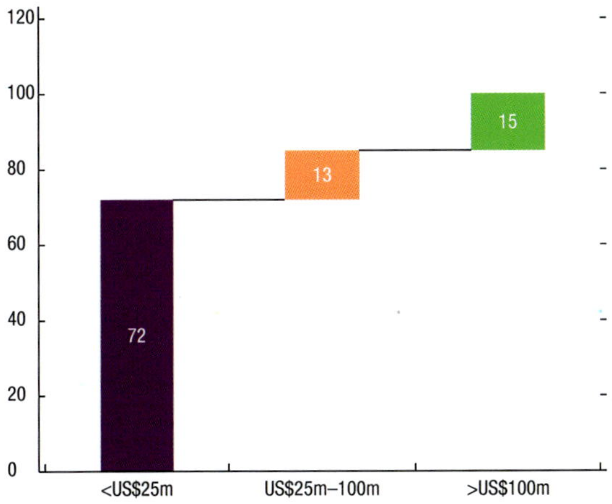

Source: Schlapinski (2018).
Note: Includes Côte d'Ivoire, Ethiopia, Ghana, Kenya, and Nigeria.

Figure 36. Africa-Focused Private Equity Fund Size
(Percent of capital raised, 2014–17)

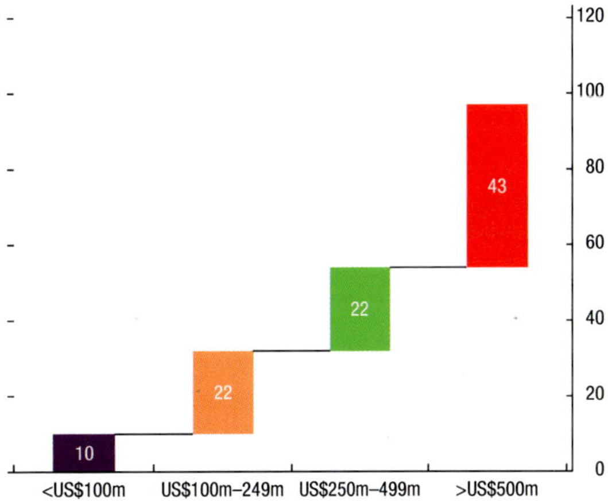

Source: Schlapinski (2018).

$100 million at all (Figure 36). In addition, investors often require an additional risk premium in the case of smaller companies to cover higher costs of sourcing, higher risk of write-offs, and missing economies of scale (IFC 2018a).

- *Lack of information available to financial investors.* In SSA, it is often challenging to get reliable data to conduct the necessary due diligence on investment projects and on-the-ground expertise is in short supply. Significant information asymmetry exists between foreign investors entering frontier markets for the first time and local companies seeking outside capital for development projects. Gathering data, finding experts in the field, and ensuring the reliability of information represent significant barriers to investment, while costs of monitoring deals can be high. This is amplified by the absence of publicly available track records of projects (IFC 2018a). Thus, private equity funds must spend more time and money in Africa originating deals and performing due diligence on their own. And operating successfully in Africa is costly and requires substantial investment in building local capability to develop and oversee the investments (Dupoux, Hammoud, and El Fihri 2016).

Enhancing the project preparation stage can significantly lower project risk and expand the pipeline of bankable projects in SSA. "Project preparation" is a wide-ranging stage of the investment management cycle (ICA 2018). It ranges from initial conception to support for deal structuring and transaction, including review of project risks, optimal risk allocation and transfer, value-for-money analysis, thorough examination of the required government support, estimations of fiscal costs and contingent liabilities, as well as efforts to secure stakeholder engagement and conduct market sounding (G20 IWG 2018).

To expand the projects' pipeline, a range of instruments have been developed to improve project preparation in LIDCs and EMEs. Among these instruments are (1) *project preparation facilities*, which cover a number of institutions specially designed for supporting development stages of investment projects (see Box 3); (2) *project development funds*, such as the South African Treasury PPP Project Development Facility, which are funds that provide financing to projects at the initial development stage with the objective of recovering costs later on[2]; and (3) *project information platforms*[3] such as the NEPAD/AUDA Program for Infrastructure Development in Africa (PIDA) in collaboration with the African Development Bank (AfDB) (AfDB 2019). In addition to these three types of instruments, some also emphasize the benefits from standardizing procedures (for example, with standard contracts) as well as developing international best practice norms (for example, international standards on infrastructure governance) to strengthen project preparation and help crowd in international investors (Collier 2014, OECD 2019a).

More generally, strong public infrastructure governance is key to reducing risks to private or semi-private projects. Because a majority of infrastructure projects with private participation in Africa are initially appraised and/or implemented in collaboration with governments (including under PPP contracts) or require complementary public assets, a strong public investment management framework is essential for optimal cooperation between public and private partners. In SSA countries, promoting high-quality public investment has long been a significant policy challenge (Barhoumi and others 2018). Having a standardized methodology and central support functions for project appraisal and risk analysis can help build a strong pipeline of investment projects, which can then be selected for financing and implementation, consistent with development priorities and with a credible medium-term framework. SSA countries should also reinforce central governments' implementation mechanisms to ensure the timely and efficient delivery of infrastructure assets. This includes enhancing the openness and transparency of procurement processes, improving the efficiency of cash management, strengthening the capacity for monitoring of the consolidated portfolio of projects, and developing infrastructure asset registries.

[2]Project development funds are revolving funds that recover the costs of project preparation directly from the agency implementing the project or from third parties such as brownfield investors interested in entering the projects. A broader definition of PPFs sometimes includes these PDFs market-driven tools.

[3]Project information platforms are databases presenting projects for investors that meet certain international standards.

Addressing Macroeconomic Risk

Macroeconomic instability is a key concern for financial investors and is a substantial part of their risk-return assessment. Economic and financial crises, large swings in economic activity, fiscal imbalances, and volatility in foreign exchange rates increase uncertainty and discourage investors by putting their returns at risk, no matter how viable individual projects may be. High inflation can also introduce volatility in relative prices and make investment a riskier and less predictable decision.

Policies that improve macroeconomic stability can foster private investment and FDI. As shown by ample economic research over the past decades, stable and steady macroeconomic conditions have a significant impact on private investment and foreign investment (see, for instance, Nonnemberg and Cardoso de Mendonça 2004; Araya, Schwartz, and Andres 2013; or Sha 2016). Private sector confidence is affected by the track record of sound macroeconomic policy (Box 4).

Addressing Exit Risk

Exit risk is another major concern for international investors. Key to building a private investor ecosystem is the ability and the range of options offered to exit investments. Financial investors realize most of the returns of projects when selling all or a part of their stakes through different channels. Buyers can be either another financial investor (who purchases the shares through initial public offerings, direct listing, or private placements, among other options); another company (sometimes called a "strategic buyer"); or the company's own management through a management buyout (Schiff and Dithrich 2018). As discussed in Chapter 3, project exit can be more complicated in Africa because of (1) illiquid and shallow financial markets; (2) weak regulatory and legal systems; and (3) capital account restrictions. The following paragraphs focus on how to alleviate these constraints.

Financial development policies can facilitate exit by increasing the liquidity of capital markets. The development of secondary markets for equity and debt allows investments to be recycled and traded at lower transaction costs.[4] Brownfield projects with a proven track record can attract potentially more risk-averse private financiers who act as secondary buyers of investment assets. Peterhoff and others (2016) describe various reforms meant to grow market liquidity in emerging markets, mainly by (1) promoting the development

[4]Innovative approaches for capital market development and financial deepening, such as the recent Joint Capital Market Program (J-CAP) launched by the World Bank and the International Finance Corporation (IFC) in 2017, can help build up liquid and stable capital markets in developing countries, leading to a more favorable exit environment for private investors.

of a diverse investor base with a focus on attracting local and international institutional investors, and enhancing retail participation; (2) increasing the pool of securities and associated financial products by increasing the number of local or foreign listings, launching derivative and exchange-traded fund products, or creating market linkages; and (3) investing in the creation of an enabling market environment through the improvement of trading technology, market, and reference data, the implementation of market-maker schemes, or developing securities lending and borrowing schemes. Within each of these three main objectives, the specific measures differ according to the level of financial sector maturity. For instance, when it comes to creating an enabling environment and reducing trade inefficiencies, Peterhoff and others (2016) advise that, at the early stage, countries concentrate on developing simple-but-efficient electronic markets, automating processes where possible, and providing a basic level of market data. As markets mature, the focus shifts toward enhancements that attract new types of investors, such as providing indices or launching market making incentive schemes.[5]

Exit risk can also be attenuated by strengthening the legal and regulatory frameworks. A set of reforms can reinforce investors' rights and ensure that property rights and contracts are enforced, legal procedures are conducted in a timely and fair manner, and taxation for investment exits is predictable (Box 5).

In addition, African countries with longstanding and extensive capital account restrictions would likely benefit from careful and gradual liberalization at a pace consistent with their institutional and financial development. In the past decade, the IMF has developed an institutional view on "capital flow liberalization"—a term that describes the removal of capital flow management measures (IMF 2012, 2013a, 2016d). Further openness to capital flows can have substantial benefits (for example, transfer of technology, more financial sector competitiveness, and lower borrowing costs) but carries also risks, such as heightened macroeconomic volatility and vulnerability to crises. In general, capital flow liberalization is more beneficial and less risky if countries have reached certain levels of financial and institutional development and if the process is supported by sound fiscal, monetary, and exchange rate policies. The appropriate degree of liberalization at any time depends on the country's circumstances and overall economic objectives; there is no presumption that full openness is an appropriate goal for all countries at all times. For countries that choose to liberalize capital flows, the process and pace need to be well planned, timed, and sequenced to ensure that its benefits outweigh the costs.

[5]For further discussion on the sequencing of reforms toward capital market development, see Karacadag, Sundararajan, and Elliott (2003); Laeven (2014); and Rojas-Suarez (2014).

Market Solutions to Insure Against these Three Risks

Some of the risks faced by financial investors can be insured or hedged against with market or government solutions. Investment guarantees, risk insurances, and hedging mechanisms are available through a number of private, government, or multilateral entities to address the needs of financial investors (both local and foreign) in developing countries (OECD 2012). These policies can cover both commercial and noncommercial (such as political) risks. For instance, the Currency Exchange Fund (TCX) was founded in 2007 by a group of DFIs, specialized microfinance investment vehicles and donors to offer solutions for managing currency risk in developing and frontier markets. These solutions, which cover more than 70 currencies, consist of financial instruments—swaps and forward contracts—that enable TCX's investors and clients to provide their borrowers with financing in their own currency, while shifting the currency risk to TCX. Another example is the political risk insurance provided by World Bank MIGA to private equity funds investing in Africa.

However, private markets to insure against specific investment risks in low-income countries can be thin or inexistent. Many risks faced by international investors in SSA countries are not easily "insurable" (Gordon 2008). First, some risks are highly idiosyncratic and cannot easily be pooled to form large-enough insurance or hedging markets. In this case, contracts need to be tailored-made and can be complex and expensive. Second, investment risks may be highly correlated (for instance, currency risks or political risks across low-income countries), so that insurers are likely to face multiple claims at the same time. Third, some triggering events may be partially under the control of the insured, particularly for political risk guarantees where actions of international investors can, to some extent, influence the likelihood of political events taking place. As a result, insurance and hedging markets may be underdeveloped, costly, or even inexistent for some types of risks. For this reason, DFIs and governments have often positioned themselves as insurers of last resort to complement private markets for customers that could not find private coverage in developing countries. In fact, many investors favor public over private schemes because they expect the official party to have more leverage to enforce the insurance contract when risks occur.

Overall, the first line of defense to reduce the risks affecting private finance flows is to create a sound business environment in recipient countries. Given the shortcomings of the risk-mitigating solutions available on the market (including their cost and scarcity), insurance and hedging tools are bound to remain second-best solutions to mitigate the risks faced by international investors in Africa. Countries should see market solutions as complementing rather than substituting for measures that address the fundamental weaknesses of policy and institutional frameworks.

Sectoral Policies: Creating a Business-Friendly Environment

The type and extent of private sector participation can vary greatly across development sectors. Between the two poles of a fully public project and a fully private project, there are numerous interim forms by which the private sector can be involved in the provision of a development project or service. Higher levels of private sector participation can occur through increased delegation of responsibility and risk. In terms of delegation of responsibility, this can range from the private sector designing, building, maintaining, operating, and/or financing a development project. The risk transfer from the public to the private sector also depends on the way in which the development project is structured with the public sector. For example, operating, commercial, and investment-related risk may be borne by either the government or the private sector entity. Below are three examples, from many different forms, of how such projects can be structured (see Figure 37):[6]

- *Management contract.* For existing assets, operation and maintenance of a project are transferred to the private sector in return of a management fee. Asset ownership and capital expenditure remains the responsibility of the public sector.
- *Lease.* Under this contract structure, the private sector operator runs the projects, retains revenues from the user, pays a lease fee to the public sector, and typically incurs significant operating and commercial risks. Overall ownership of the asset remains with the contracting authority.
- *Concession.* In this case, the private sector takes responsibility for the full development of a project in return for payment from either the government or the user. Full development includes designing, building, financing, operating, and maintaining the project.

The desired level of private sector engagement within a sector or in a specific project depends on five key considerations. While increased private sector engagement can bring in additional financing and other benefits, the extent of involvement depends on the characteristics of each development sector and, more precisely, each project within the sector. Applying the following five considerations helps to identify the "natural habitat" of development

[6]See description of the possible arrangements in Farquharson and others (2011), World Bank (2017a), and Yescombe (2017).

Figure 37. The Public-Private Continuum

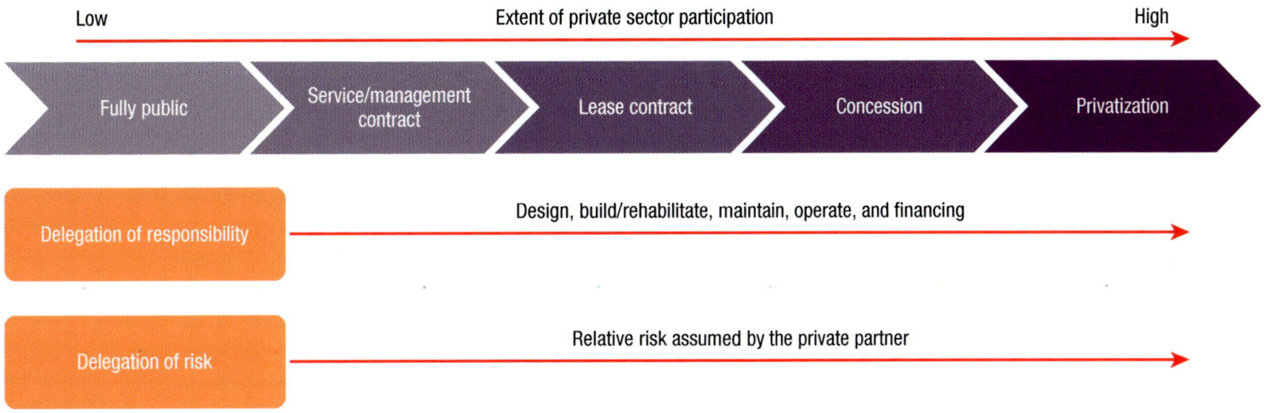

Source: World Bank (2017a).

projects along the continuum from a fully public to fully private project (Figure 38):[7]

- *Ability to generate private returns* (Annex 1). Does the project generate sufficient risk-adjusted profits and over a period of time that is not excessively long? For example, will the private sector be able to charge user fees to cover costs and make an adequate return?
- *Externality gap.* Is the social return sufficiently larger than the private return resulting in a large externality gap that leads to under provision by the private sector and justifies a greater role for the public sector (Jaffe 1998)?
- *Risk transfer.* Is the private partner willing to accept and manage efficiently project risks related to financial, technical, and operational issues?
- *Efficiency.* To what extent does the private sector have more expertise to manage projects or deliver services and will this generate efficiency gains, including in light of possible transaction costs?
- *Equity.* Will access and coverage be sufficient to meet social objectives?

The scope for private sector engagement is higher in major parts of the electricity and transportation sectors. Based on the five key considerations, power generation and highways are better suited for private sector engagement. They are projects in which the private sector has expertise, is willing to accept risks, can generate private returns (through toll roads, for instance), and can meet

[7]Financing constraints are also an important factor. This section, including Figure 38, assumes that neither the public sector nor the private sector is overleveraged; thus, the choice of the natural habitat is unconstrained. In practice, some parts of the continuum may not be accessible.

Figure 38. The "Natural Habitat" of Development Projects along the Public-Private Continuum

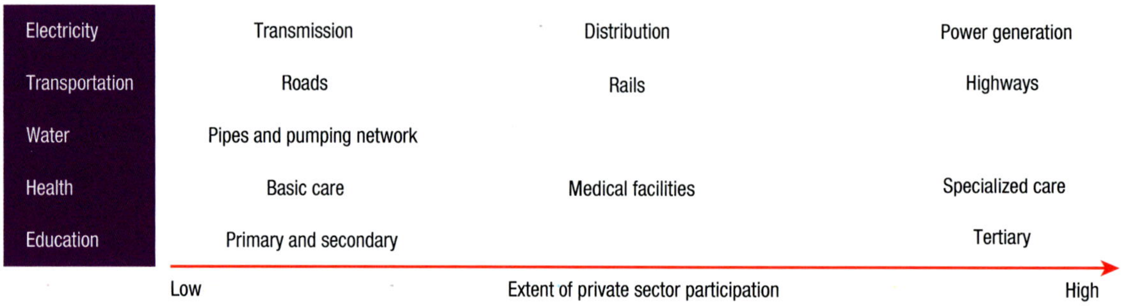

Source: IMF staff.
Note: The figure provides illustrative examples to show the diversity of private sector involvement within sectors rather than a comprehensive and precise categorization.

social and equity objectives. This contrasts with basic healthcare and primary and secondary education where the social objective of universal access may be at odds with the ability of the private sector to generate private returns, and a large externality gap is likely.[8]

Sectoral policies have an important role to play in bringing in the desired level of private sector engagement. Although a case can be made for more private sector participation in some development projects, in practice, actual levels of participation are limited. For example, in SSA half of all countries have not engaged the private sector in electricity generation or distribution (Foster and others 2017). The reasons for this limited participation often relate to broader macroeconomic factors (highlighted at the beginning of this chapter), but contributory factors also exist at the sectoral level. Thus, policies needed to bring in more private investment also have a sectoral dimension and have to be tailored to the specificities of each sector, as illustrated by successful projects carried out in the region (Box 6). Annex 4 describes some examples of measures recommended in the five main areas covered by the paper (road, water, electricity, education, and health). Nonetheless, some common principles are relevant for all sectoral policies:

- *Price-setting mechanisms that enable cost recovery.* In cases where the end-user is paying directly for the provision of the service or access to infrastructure, it is essential that the pricing mechanism allows for cost recovery. The price mechanism should reflect input costs, and existing price subsidies should

[8]For the same reasons, private sector participation proved easiest in the telecommunications sector in the 1990s and 2000s. Tertiary education is another example where private sector participation is high with an average enrollment of 30 percent in private institutions in sub-Saharan Africa (based on reporting countries in EdStats).

be phased out (IMF 2013b). In the electricity, water, and transportation sectors, this means that tariffs or tolls should be set at a level that creates sufficient returns and that there is scope to change prices.[9] Often, political and social pressures to ensure some basic services, such as water, are affordable to large proportions of the poor keep prices at too low a level, which can result in accumulation of losses or reliance on inefficient public subsidies. In such cases, the introduction of cost-recovery price mechanisms may need to be accompanied by social transfers, provided in a transparent and targeted way.

- *Regulations that provide a conducive framework for the private sector to operate.* Sectoral regulations are needed to provide the framework through which the private sector can participate in the creation and delivery of development services. Often regulatory changes are needed to remove barriers to entry to a particular sector or to streamline procedures. For example, legislation may restrict the provision of electricity or services such as education solely to the public sector. In some countries, a single piece of legislation can cover all sectors or sector-specific legislation can be developed. Often, this legislation can be conceived in consultation with the private sector, drawing on the experiences of other countries.
- *Transparent public sector governance.* In most development sectors, the private provider often operates closely with the state or other state-owned entities. For example, in the electricity sector, state-owned enterprises in charge of distribution often buy electricity from private power producers. This creates an onus on ensuring that the institutional framework and governance of the sector provides a transparent operating framework in which rules can be enforced, often in the form of an independent regulatory body. Moreover, the governance and management of state-owned enterprises should ensure they are run efficiently and avoid creating negative spillovers to the private sector.
- *Adequate provision of complementary inputs.* Even in projects or sectors for which there is a clear case for private sector involvement, the public sector still needs to ensure that complementary factors of production are available to help overcome coordination failures. For example, this could include helping to bring in personnel with the appropriate skillset to be able to develop PPPs and liaise between the public and private sector. The specificities will vary depending on the project but in general, it requires the state to be aware and responsive to the needs of the private sector provider.

Technological advancements are also transforming the development landscape, creating the potential for a larger role for the private sector. New technologies and digital connectivity are helping to lower costs and increase

[9]For more details see, for instance, Coady and others (2012).

access, both of which could create potential for more private sector provision of development services. For example, in the electricity sector, the innovation of mini-grids using solar power is already bringing low-cost electricity to unconnected areas (ESMAP 2019). The use of mobile money is also allowing for remote bill payment, producing much improved collection rates (IMF 2019a). The health and education sectors are becoming increasingly digitalized through the use of remote diagnosis and learning opportunities (Broadband Commission 2019). While the implications of such technological changes are evolving, it will be important to review and adapt sectoral level policies to help countries benefit from these advances and manage emerging risks.

Box 3. Project Preparation Facilities

Project preparation facilities (PPFs) support governments, investors, and developers of infrastructure projects by helping them to expedite the technical, financial, legal, and regulatory processes (USAID 2016). PPFs are generally established by multilateral financial institutions and other donors. PPFs include grant-based facilities financed by donors as well as more commercially oriented facilities that have to recover at least part of their costs.

PPFs help bridge the gap from conceptualization and feasibility analyses to deal structuring and transaction support. PPFs cover various aspects of the project throughout the construction and early operations stages (GIH 2018). They may provide technical and/or financial supports to project owners or concessionaires in the project preparation and help them improve the efficacy of preparation practices with the eventual goal of reducing considerably the time span from project development to financial closure. Such support can cover a wide range of activities, including undertaking project feasibility studies, such as value-for-money analysis; developing procurement documents and project concessional agreements; undertaking social and environmental studies; and creating awareness among the main stakeholders. PPFs can also provide financial assistance to local governments or special public sector agencies to support the financial, legal, and technical advisory services required to facilitate private investment into infrastructure projects. This assistance is integral to creating bankable projects.

PPFs can crowd in project finance, but their impact has so far been limited. Evidence suggests that PPFs have an impact on private investment, helping generate projects that would not have come to fruition without them (G20 IWG 2018). However, PPFs are still too small in scale to decisively unlock the resources needed to fill the investment gap in SDG sectors (WEF 2016, G20 2017). About 20 PPFs have been operating in Africa alone in recent years. A notable one is the AfDB grant-based NEPAD Infrastructure Project Preparation Facility (NEPAD-IPPF) with a volume of funds about $110 million in 2020. It focuses on three SDG-relevant sectors: energy, transportation, and water. Since its inception it has approved about 100 projects for regional infrastructure projects, resulting in a crowding in of private investment of more than $24 billion according to the AfDB (AfDB 2019). Another hurdle is that existing PPFs in Africa often fall short in committing their resources because of lack of suitable projects that meet their eligibility criteria (Kortekaas 2015).

In recent years DFIs have significantly scaled up their engagement in project preparation. For example, the newly established US International Development Corporation (DFC)—which merged the US governmental DFI, the Overseas Private Investment Corporation, with parts of the US Agency for International Development credit facilities in 2019—will significantly extend the US private sector support capacity to up to

Box 3. Project Preparation Facilities *(continued)*

$60 billion worldwide, including a grant window for feasibility studies. Other initiatives from DFIs, such as Choose Africa by the French Development Agency and AfricaGrow/AfricaConnect and Business Network Africa by the German Investment and Development Corporation, also provide support for project preparation.

Box 4. Policies for Macroeconomic Stability and Resilience in Low-Income Countries

Well-designed, prudent, and sustainable government and central bank policies can foster macroeconomic stability:

- *Monetary policy.* African countries should strive to develop a coherent, transparent, and forward-looking monetary policy framework. IMF (2015b) identifies a number of best principles in this area. In particular, the central bank should have a clear mandate that assigns primacy to the goal of price stability, and it should follow a forward-looking strategy that promotes that goal while fostering macroeconomic and financial stability. An explicit inflation objective should serve as the cornerstone for monetary policy actions and communications. The central bank's procedures for implementing monetary policy should be framed in terms of a specific short-term interest rate. Such objectives and operating procedures can lower inflation, reduce interest rate volatility, and promote financial market development.
- *Exchange rate policy.* Sound foreign exchange reserve management can substantially contain risks for investors by reducing exchange rate volatility. Reserve management strategies should comply with best international principles, including maintaining adequate buffers, ensuring the liquidity of reserves, managing risks prudently when placing reserves, and complying with transparency standards (IMF 2016b). The level of "adequate" reserves can be assessed through various tools, including simple metrics and more complex cost-benefit models (IMF 2016c).
- *Fiscal policy.* Well-managed public finances can improve sovereign risk ratings and build investor's confidence in the ability of government to deliver on core state functions. Fiscal discipline is essential to containing debt vulnerabilities while protecting outlays that are key to growth prospects (IMF 2018b, 2019b). In African countries, some priorities to enhance fiscal resilience include diversifying the revenue sources by gradually increasing taxes from bases other than commodities; building fiscal buffers, where possible, to provide space for countercyclical fiscal policies when the economy is hit by shocks; adopting prudent debt management practices; enhancing expenditure efficiency; and strengthening public financial management, including the oversight of state-owned enterprises, to mitigate the occurrence of contingent liabilities.

Box 5. Best Practices to Strengthen Legal Frameworks for Investor Protection

Investor protection frameworks are meant to shield investors against numerous risks. To simplify, risks can be grouped into three main categories: (1) the *protection of minority shareholders against majority shareholders* measures the rights and legal protections of minority shareholders against unfair treatment afforded under the law that companies must abide by; (2) the *protection of investors against directors* describes safeguards against directors' misuse of corporate assets for personal gain; and (3) the *protection of investors against policy instability* captures various types of risks related to government actions, including risks of expropriation, breach of government contractual payment obligations, or unexpected and frequent changes in laws and regulations.

Protection Against Majority Shareholders

International experience shows that the protection of minority shareholders can be strengthened by complying with a few core principles. These include (1) ensuring adequate shareholder rights and role in major corporate decisions; (2) facilitating access to corporate documents; and (3) requiring greater corporate transparency regarding activities and transactions and clarifying ownership and control structures.

In recent years, several countries have conducted successful reforms in this area. For instance, in 2019 Sudan gave minority shareholders a more prominent role in major corporate decisions such as major transactions, issuance of new shares, and appointments of auditors. In 2019, China increased minority shareholders rights and role in major corporate decisions, and mandated corporations to provide more information on control structures.

Protection Against Directors

Legal reforms can strengthen the protection of investors against directors and managers. Best practices include (1) requiring pre-approval safeguards for transactions with interested parties (for example, shareholder consultation and review by an independent auditor), (2) ensuring shareholders' ability to sue and hold directors accountable for self-dealing, (3) ensuring that a court can set aside transactions upon a successful claim by shareholders, and (4) providing disclosure of business activities in periodic filings (for example, through annual reports).

Investor protection has recently been strengthened in a number of African countries. In 2019, Djibouti strengthened investor protections by modifying its Code of Commerce as well as its Code of Civil Procedure; the amendments provide that related-party transactions must be approved by companies' general assembly meeting excluding interested members, and that an interested director can be held liable when the transaction is unfair or prejudicial to the other shareholders. In 2018, Kenya passed a legislation

Box 5. Best Practices to Strengthen Legal Frameworks for Investor Protection *(continued)*

that increased corporate transparency requirements. The law gives more agenda-setting power to shareholders and discloses board members activities in other companies, executive compensation, and audit reports.

Protection Against Policy Instability

Investors need assurances that the institutional and policy framework will remain relatively stable and predictable and that the authorities will not abuse their position as rule maker. Some safeguards can include (1) using the national justice system to start the complaint (for example through courts) in case of dispute with the authorities; (2) launching a claim procedure with the International Center for Settlements of Investment Disputes (ICSID) of the World Bank, and (3) making use of the World Bank guarantee products (for example the IDA Partial Risk Guarantee (PRG) or Multilateral Investment Guarantee Agency (MIGA) guarantee).

Some countries are taking steps to create a more stable and predictable environment. The 2014 investment code of the Kingdom of Jordan includes dispute settlement provisions that give foreign investors access to arbitration in the event of a dispute with the authorities, for instance, protection from expropriation, breach of contract, as well as a guarantee of free transfer of capital and profits. In addition, the 2015 investment code of Rwanda introduced provisions that any dispute arising between a foreign investor and one or more public organs in connection with a registered investment enterprise shall be amicably settled; when an amicable settlement cannot be reached, parties shall refer the dispute to an arbitration agency as agreed on in a written agreement between both parties.

Box 6. Successful Sectoral Policies and Projects in Africa

This box provides examples of recent projects across sub-Saharan Africa that illustrate the ways through which the private sector can help deliver development projects in the region. In each case, sectoral policies played an important role in creating the frameworks needed to enable the private sector to operate.

Toll Road in Senegal

Senegal is one of the first countries (outside of South Africa) to successfully develop a PPP toll road in sub-Saharan Africa. The Dakar-Diamniadio toll highway was created in response to the existing highway, which lacked capacity for existing travel needs and had minimal scope for increasing capacity for the rapidly expanding city. The PPP phases of the construction occurred between December 2006 and August 2013. Because this was Senegal's first PPP, longer timelines and costs emerged as a result of the need to establish and refine the framework and for necessary startup tasks, such as training staff. Key factors that contributed to its success include: early creation of an effective legislative and institutional framework ahead of the procurement process; establishment of a well-resourced PPP unit to prepare and manage the process; advanced communications touting the benefits of the highway; and existence of an un-tolled version, which helped to reduce criticism and protests in response to the toll. In addition, strong political support at the highest levels ensured that the concession agency was sufficiently empowered (Brocklebank 2014).

Power Plant in Rwanda

The Kivu 56 Power Plant project draws methane from the bottom of Lake Kivu as fuel for power generation in an environmentally friendly and sustainable manner. Importantly, because the buildup of methane below the lake could lead to dangerous gas eruptions, the extraction of the methane reduces a potential danger. The Government of Rwanda agreed to a 25-year power-purchase agreement and secured debt and equity financing from private and official creditors as well as a political risk guarantee by the World Bank Group Multilateral Investment Guarantee Agency. Although the project faced numerous financing and construction setbacks, after a change in investors in 2008 the project was completed in 2015. This complex PPP project received high-level political commitment, especially in the early stages. The fact that it faced construction and financing challenges and was one of the country's first PPP projects led to the government learning important lessons on how to manage PPPs (Yescombe 2017).

Renewable Energy in South Africa

Launched by South Africa in 2011, the Renewable Energy Independent Power Producer Procurement Program (REIPPPP) has been successful in bringing in investment

Box 6. Successful Sectoral Policies and Projects in Africa *(continued)*

and expertise from the private sector to boost energy production at competitive prices. The first round of bidding attracted a spectrum of domestic and international investors. Prices fell in successive rounds, and projects came on stream in just two years. Much of the success has been attributed to an experienced project management team with PPP expertise, a sufficiently large program and structure to attract multiple competitive bids, and a conducive global environment for renewable energy. More broadly, the experience demonstrates the importance of a well-designed and transparent procurement process that offers reasonable rates of return where the government mitigates key risks (Eberhard, Kolker, and Leighland 2014).

CHAPTER

5 Government Incentives: Needed but Costly and Risky?

Although a critical step, creating a business-friendly environment in and of itself may not be sufficient. Many African countries have made tangible progress in improving their business climate but still struggle to attract private finance because of market failures, which are widespread in development sectors. In this situation, governments may need to provide direct incentives to investors to encourage them to finance private or semi-private projects. This chapter discusses the experience with such incentives and how they should be designed to be most effective and least costly.

Market Failures in Development Sectors

Market failures are prevalent in development sectors. The term "market failures" denotes economic situations wherein the allocation of goods and services in a free market is inefficient and their provision by the private sector is structurally insufficient. Compared to other types of capital, infrastructure is more likely to be subject to market failures for three main reasons (IMF 2014). First, many infrastructure projects often entail large, capital-intensive investments and, therefore, tend to be "natural monopolies," which means that it is more cost-effective for services to be provided by a single entity. Second, projects have significant upfront costs, but the returns accrue over long periods of time, often several decades, and may be difficult to assess over such a long horizon. Third, infrastructure investments generate positive externalities, so that the social return of a project for the whole population can exceed the private returns generated for the investor.

Market failures can significantly reduce the pool of private finance. Indeed, they constrain the ability of financial investors to generate or appropriate private returns. Table 4 summarizes some of the main mechanisms. Because of these market features, the risk-adjusted returns of development projects

Table 4. Examples of Market Failures in Development Sectors

Project Characteristics	Impact on Private Finance
Large upfront costs	Investors may be unable to frontload financing.
Long period for project preparation, procurement, and construction of assets (before starting operations)	Most financial investors have a short-term horizon, which may conflict with the need to provide long-term/stable financing in illiquid assets.
Low and uncertain returns, at least in the first stages of a project	Uncertainty about returns (for example, capacity to implement water tariff revisions) may discourage investors.
Externalities	Private investors rarely take into account social returns.
Need to ensure universal and equitable access to services, which means that prices cannot fully reflect market forces. A related issue is the affordability constraint (low ability of customers to pay).	Limits the ability to apply cost-recovery prices for services. Prices are often highly regulated and may be too low to satisfy return requirements of financial investors.
Natural monopoly; low competition	Natural monopolies are likely to use market power to prevent the entry of new players. Natural monopolies are also associated with high fixed costs, which reduces returns.
Asymmetries of information between the entity managing/implementing the project and financial investors	Lack of transparency may discourage investors.
Coordination failures	When projects and firms are organized across clusters and value chains, investors may have little incentive to be the first to enter markets and sectors in which these networks are inexistent or too small. Pioneer investors are likely to be penalized.
Public goods with high risk of free riding (for example, ecosystem and biodiversity protection)	Investors may not be able to recoup service costs if consumers unwilling to pay can still access the service or goods.

Source: IMF staff.

may be structurally too low and unappealing to investors even in a "perfect" business environment. Partly for this reason, social and physical infrastructures have historically been mostly provided by the public sector or regulated private entities (see Chapter 2).

Market failures are often sector or even project specific. Market failures materialize in multiple and idiosyncratic ways. They affect primary education differently from tertiary education. And education displays different distortions from electricity distribution or highway construction. For instance, UN (2018) provides a detailed analysis of the water and sanitation sector, showing that very specific constraints limit the participation of private producers. One peculiarity of this sector: it is not economically viable to build competing sets of pipes for the network infrastructure, which severely limits competitive pressures on providers. In addition, even more than for other types of infrastructure, access to water and sanitation must be provided to all households regardless of their ability to pay. As a result, water tariffs are heavily regulated. Another characteristic of water and sanitation services is that they are usually locally provided (at the municipal level), which limits the scope for wider-scale networks and economies of scale. All these factors make private involvement more difficult and elusive in water provision.

Market failures can justify the use of public incentives to attract more financing to private projects. The market failure argument is generally used to justify the public provision of physical and social infrastructure. However, as discussed at the beginning of the paper, fiscal space is highly constrained in

Africa at the moment. By lifting the risk-adjusted returns of private projects, the hope is that public incentives could unlock significant amounts of private finance and achieve similar (or better) development outcomes than under traditional public procurement at a lower budgetary cost. The next section approaches this question within a theoretical model, whereas the final section discusses some practical considerations on the efficient design of public incentives.

Cost-Benefit Analysis of Public Interventions: A Model-Based Analysis

Governments face a fundamental question: how should they allocate their scarce resources to development projects? As discussed in Chapter 2, the large increase in public debt in recent years combined with lingering difficulties to mobilize domestic revenue have reduced the budgetary space available to African governments to finance transformational investments in social and physical infrastructure—investments that are typically costly and complex and require a long time to implement. This has significantly raised the bar for governments to allocate their funds in the most efficient way.

A trade-off can emerge in deciding to use these resources to either fund public investment or promote private investment. In the last decade, a policy debate has arisen as to whether public funds could have higher leverage if used to incentivize private investment rather than to finance governments' projects. This debate occurred simultaneously in various contexts, including the response to the global financial crisis (for instance, European investment plans) and rethinking donor financing modalities (for example, blending initiatives). The intuition is that, when one dollar of public incentive is used to unlock private investment, it could have a "multiplier effect" and generate higher levels of development services than under the traditional approach of public expenditure.

In the context of a macroeconomic model, the authors characterize this trade-off by comparing three stylized scenarios. These three scenarios describe alternative ways of investing public resources and capture, in a simplified way, the essence of the trade-offs faced by governments (Figure 39). The first scenario describes the traditional model of infrastructure financing (at least, in low-income countries) wherein funds are invested in development projects through the central government budget or SOEs.[1] The second scenario uses the public funds to lower the private sector's production costs through an investment subsidy, which, in the model, encapsulates, in a stylized way, various forms of government incentives that improve the risk-adjusted return

[1]In both cases, development projects have a fiscal cost, either directly as a budget program carried out by a line ministry or indirectly in the form of a government transfer to a SOE.

Figure 39. Allocation of Public Funds

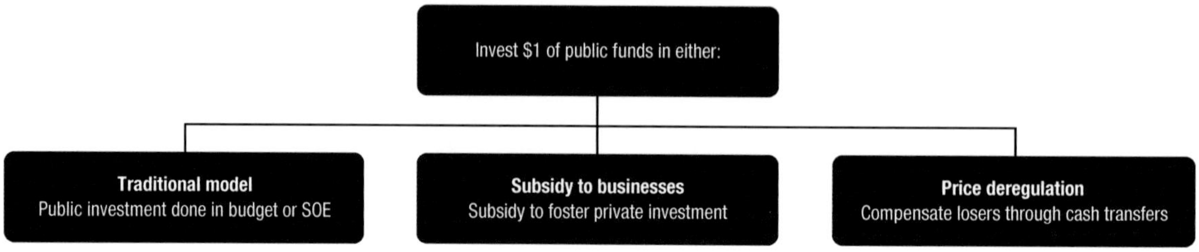

Source: IMF staff.
Note: SOE = state-owned enterprise.

of the private sector (including guarantees and other types of subsidies and grants). Finally, the third scenario assumes liberalization of the service prices, which also fosters private investment—this time not by reducing costs but by raising private returns. In the third scenario, public funds are used to compensate the poor through targeted cash transfers, since the price increase reduces their purchasing power. Of course, the real world is a mix of these three options. But these stylized scenarios can illustrate fundamental decisions to be made by governments.

Main Aspects of the Macroeconomic Model

To better understand and quantify these trade-offs, the authors use a multisector general equilibrium model tailored to developing economies. This allows for tracing out and quantifying the channels by which investment may affect inequality, poverty, and growth. The model can be used to assess the impact of alternative policies, taking into account the fact that the government needs to finance them through higher taxes or lower expenditure. A sketch of the model can be found in Annex 5. The principal features of the model include (1) significant role for commodities, with exports heavily concentrated in these sectors; (2) a relatively small manufacturing sector; (3) a relatively large public sector; (4) a basic financial sector with limited opportunities for risk sharing; and (5) households subject to shocks, which affect their incomes. With these components, the model can also take into account the economy's income distribution.

The model is applied to the electricity sector, which displays several key characteristics of development projects. Like most other development services, electricity is a consumption good, but it is also an input used for the production of other goods, in the same way as water, roads, health, and education are key ingredients for potential growth. Economic prospects can be undermined when these are scarce or unequally distributed. Another interesting characteristic of electricity is that prices are often regulated to guarantee broad access to the population. A feature of most development-related services is that their prices are generally set below cost-recovery levels, making their production less attractive to the private sector.

To illustrate the current challenges of low-income countries, the analysis starts with a baseline scenario characterized by a situation of rationing attributed to market failures. In the baseline, all electricity is produced by the public sector—either directly from the general government or from a SOE—and it is insufficient.[2] Prices are assumed to be regulated and maintained at a relatively low level, allowing poor populations to have some access to services. However, given that the government's interventions are constrained by high public debt and difficulty in raising taxes, it cannot fully satisfy the demand for electricity of households and businesses at the regulated price. Because the production of energy is insufficient, both poor and rich populations are rationed out. It is assumed that rationing affects more severely households at the upper brackets of the income distribution and the industrial sector. These two groups have the means to pay and would see improvements in their welfare by purchasing more energy at the prevailing price, but they cannot obtain it. At the same time, because of the low regulated prices, the private sector has little incentive to come in as a supplier of this service.

The three scenarios depart from this initial rationing situation in different ways. It is assumed that the government can spend at the margin a fixed amount of money in three alternative ways. Scenario 1 uses the funds for more public delivery of electricity. Scenarios 2 and 3 use the funds to incentivize the private sector to produce more electricity and/or compensate the losers of the reform. The following paragraphs describe the scenarios in greater detail.

The Three Scenarios

Scenario 1 raises energy production further through the traditional framework of public provision. In practice, this scenario could be described as "business as usual," meaning that the government would continue to produce electricity but with more money. In the context of the model, this scenario is implemented by assuming that the public funds are used by the government to purchase imported energy (rather than to produce more domestic energy).[3] We also assume that the additional energy is imported at the interna-

[2]The model takes as given the situation of rationing, without explicitly linking it to a specific market failure. Some of the arguments described in Table 4 could provide justifications for the absence of private production under the baseline.

[3]The import assumption is to keep the analysis simpler. Importantly, this assumption does not place Scenario 1 at a disadvantage relative to the other scenarios when it comes to comparing GDP outcomes. Indeed, increases in domestic production of energy by the public sector would require resources that the government

tional price, which exceeds the domestic price of the baseline by 10 percent (in case the additional energy were to be produced domestically rather than imported, results would be broadly similar, including on output, since the increase in marginal costs of production would also make domestic production more expensive than under the baseline).[4] In this scenario, the government still charges the low domestic price to consumers despite the higher cost of energy provision. Importantly, it is assumed that productivity is similar under the baseline and Scenario 1, which means that the government continues to deliver electricity as inefficiently as before. Reforms meant to boost SOE efficiency are not factored in, although the authors discuss below how they could affect the results.

Scenario 2 considers an investment subsidy in the energy sector, which directly lowers the cost of capital and fosters the private production of energy. Specifically, the investment subsidy reduces the marginal cost of capital (equal to the interest rate minus the subsidy rate), directly encouraging investment at the margin. It is worth mentioning that this subsidy is very different from the type of poorly designed and distortionary subsidy discussed in the fuel subsidy literature, such as Coady and others (2010). This second form of subsidy is generally computed as adjustment factor in a formula setting the domestic price of fuel, leaving all components of the formula unchanged, including the margins of importers, distributors, and retailers. When international prices go up (respectively down), the fuel subsidy increases (respectively decreases) to keep the retail price constant. Contrary to the investment subsidy modeled here, the fuel subsidy tends to annihilate any profit maximization behavior on the part of the operators and greatly reduces their incentive to invest in new capacity. In fact, the investment subsidy that this chapter models is closer to what the tax literature calls a "cost-based incentive," which has good properties in terms of efficiency (see IMF 2015a).

Scenario 3 allows energy prices to increase in the context of a deregulation. By allowing energy prices to go up, Scenario 3 increases the private sector's profitability of investing in the energy sector and boosts production. Since higher energy prices affect the purchasing power of the poor, targeted cash transfers are also included as part of the policy package. In the cases consid-

should obtain from the private sector (in the form of current or future higher taxes). Assuming, instead, that public provision comes from imports gives in fact Scenario 1 an advantage regarding its impact on GDP, as the cost of each additional unit of energy provided remains constant (equal to the international price). If domestic production were to be used, as marginal costs increase, then the amount of resources taken from the private sector and used in the SOE, would be larger and the drop in GDP likely to be larger.

[4]Domestic prices are controlled by the state to make some energy available to low-income households; thus, the international price is expected to be higher than the domestic price. The ad hoc 10 percent gap between import prices and domestic prices is probably a very conservative assumption. Underpricing is widespread in the energy sector. For instance, Coady and others (2019) show that country-level coal prices were below half of their fully efficient levels in 2015, while road fuel prices fell short of their efficient levels by 20 percent.

ered here, the size of the cash transfers is calibrated to exactly compensate the poor for their loss in purchasing power as energy prices change.[5]

To anchor all scenarios, it is assumed that the cost for the government is identical across the three cases and financed through higher consumption taxes.[6] In Scenario 1, the government spends 1 percent of GDP to increase energy provision by importing the additional energy. In Scenario 2, the government provides an investment subsidy to private energy producers equivalent to 1 percent of GDP. In Scenario 3, energy prices are allowed to increase. This has no direct cost to the government but, given that the poor are negatively affected, the government increases its cash transfers by 1 percent of GDP (targeted to poor households and exactly the size needed so that in equilibrium their purchasing power is unaffected by the higher energy price). In all three scenarios, consumption taxes are employed to raise revenues by 1 percent of GDP, since these taxes tend to be the least distortive on macroeconomic performance. Because it is a general equilibrium model, the effect of economic activity is taken into account; this means that, to increase tax revenues by 1 percent of GDP, tax rates do not increase identically across all scenarios. In addition, given that the calculations are done in equilibrium, the model accounts for the distortionary effects on consumption and output that higher tax rates may create; thus, the capacity of the government to increase energy production may be limited by its ability to mobilize additional revenues.

The three scenarios are then compared in terms of their growth and income distribution outcomes. By assumption, the model uses the same amount of public funds across the three scenarios and analyzes how alternative ways of allocating these funds can affect production and income. Importantly, both the use of funds (for example, for public investment, subsidy, or cash transfers to the poor) as well as the way these are financed (for example, through various forms of taxation) can have implications for efficiency and equity. The model takes into account the two dimensions.

[5]The price of electricity is deregulated and adjusted upward in Scenario 3 until two conditions are met: (1) the purchasing power of the poor is unchanged compared to the baseline, and (2) the budgetary cost of the government intervention reaches 1 percent of GDP (as in the other scenarios). As a result, deregulation is only partial in Scenario 3, and the price cannot fully reach cost-recovery (but it is still higher than under the baseline). Full cost-recovery would be too costly for the government and exceed the budgetary envelope allowed under the scenario to finance cash transfers to the poor. In the calibrated model, the domestic price of Scenario 3 happens to increase by 10 percent relative to baseline.

[6]The simulations are based on a fixed budgetary cost expressed as GDP ratio to be able to interpret the results in an intuitive way. Doing the simulations with a fixed nominal amount of public spending across scenarios (for example, $1), instead of a fixed GDP ratio (for example, 1 percent of GDP), would not change the main findings of this section, since GDP is not dramatically affected by the experiments.

Figure 40. Real Energy Units
(Percent change relative to baseline)

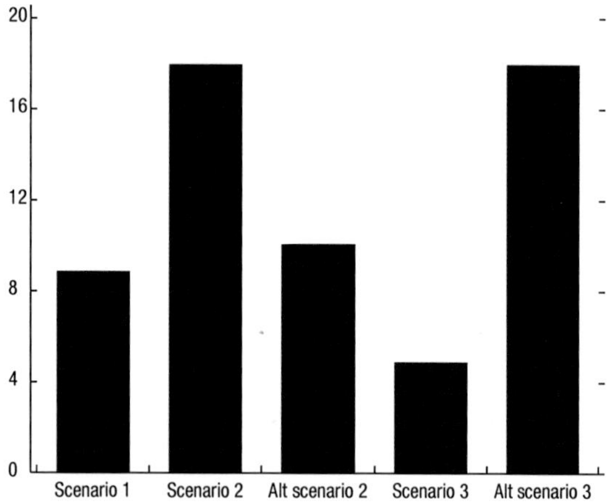

Source: IMF staff simulations.

Main Findings

Energy use increases much more in Scenario 2 than in the other scenarios. In the calibrated economy considered here, the 1 percent of GDP investment subsidy of Scenario 2 delivers an increase in energy used of close to 20 percent in real terms relative to baseline (Figure 40).[7] This is about twice as high as what is achieved in Scenarios 1 and 3. Indeed, the investment subsidy has a "multiplier effect," in the sense that it increases the provision of energy services much more than if the same amount had been used by the government to import energy. By comparison, the effect on energy use is lower under Scenario 1 (due to the higher cost of imported energy) and Scenario 3 (because the cost of compensating the poor is elevated and a budget of 1 percent of GDP allows for only a modest price increase).[8]

However, this result depends on the critical assumption that the total factor productivity (TFP) of the energy sector is unaffected by the change in policy. The empirical literature on private sector participation shows that the deregulation of prices is frequently associated with productivity gains in the energy sector (Harris 2003, Andres and others 2008, Gassner, Popov, and Pushak 2009, Estache and Philippe 2012, Estrin and Pelletier 2018, Foster and Rana 2020). To incorporate the productivity effect, the authors build alternative versions of Scenarios 2 and 3. Regarding Scenario 2, its superior performance is essentially based on the "perfect" design of the subsidy, which closes the gap between costs and returns without hurting productivity. In reality, subsidies are often poorly targeted, benefiting firms that do not need them. In the context of the model, this poor targeting can be implemented by assuming

[7]Note that domestic production and domestic use may differ since the model includes imports.

[8]As explained in footnote 5, Scenario 3 is a scenario of "partial liberalization" of prices. An alternative way to calibrate this experiment would be to allow prices to increase so as to maximize energy produced and used ("full liberalization") and let the purchasing power of the poor deteriorate (while cushioning part of it by providing 1 percent of GDP of targeted transfers). In terms of energy production and GDP, the impact would be still lower than Scenario 2 as higher energy prices quickly diminish the desired amounts of energy. The distributional consequences would naturally be much worse, with entrepreneurs benefiting greatly at the expense of the rest of the economy and, in particular, poor households.

Figure 41. Real GDP
(Percent change relative to baseline)

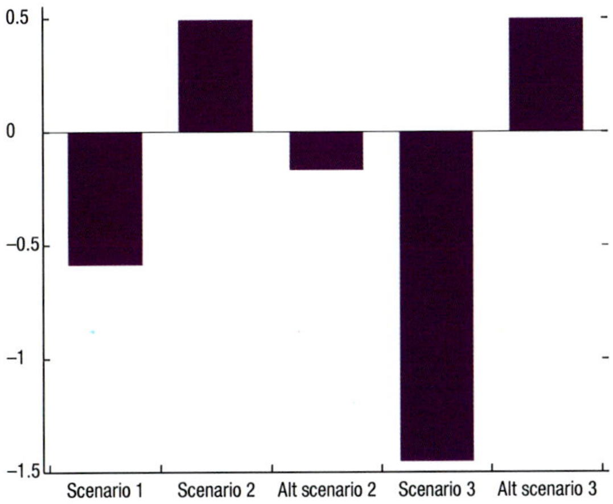

Source: IMF staff simulations.

Figure 42. Sectoral Real Value Added
(Percent change relative to baseline)

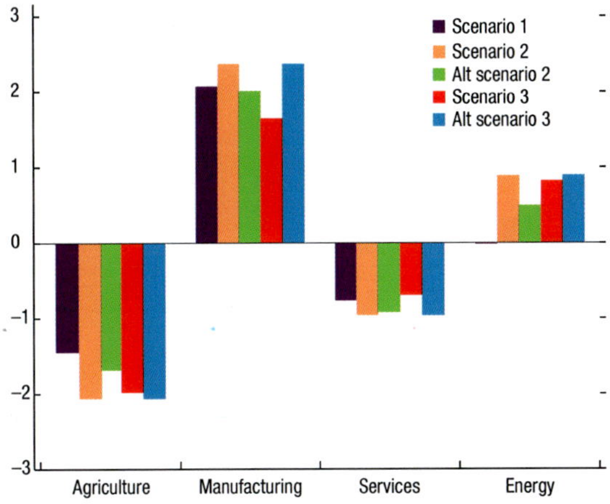

Source: IMF staff simulations.

that productivity is negatively affected by the subsidy.[9] Thus, the authors model an alternative version of Scenario 2 that assumes a 10 percent decline in the TFP level in the energy sector (relative to baseline). Under this realistic assumption, a large part of the benefits of Scenario 2 would evaporate. By contrast, liberalizing energy prices under Scenario 3 may increase sectoral productivity. To consider this possibility, a modified version of Scenario 3 with higher productivity is considered. In the calibrated economy, the TFP of the energy sector would have to increase by at least 12 percent (relative to baseline) to match the positive impact of Scenario 2 in terms of energy use. If the TFP level increased by more than 12 percent, the modified Scenario 3 would dominate Scenario 2. Note that the overall range for productivity levels delineated by the two modified scenarios seems reasonable given empirical evidence—about 20 percentage points, equally distributed around the baseline. In fact, the productivity gap between environments with inefficient subsidies versus deregulated prices could be even higher.

From a growth perspective, Scenario 2 is the only scenario with a positive impact on GDP, under the assumption of unchanged productivity. The scenarios are compared in terms of their impact on sectoral and aggregate growth (Figures 41 and 42). The baseline and each scenario have different growth outcomes depending on whether three types of frictions are more or less present: (1) the degree of energy rationing (since more availability of energy is good for producers in all sectors and thus for growth); (2) the

[9]A less-perfectly designed investment subsidy can indeed lower TFP. For example, if incumbent firms use the money to deter possible entrants and maintain a monopoly, then productivity would be below the production possibility frontier.

Figure 43. Welfare Impact
(Percent change relative to baseline)

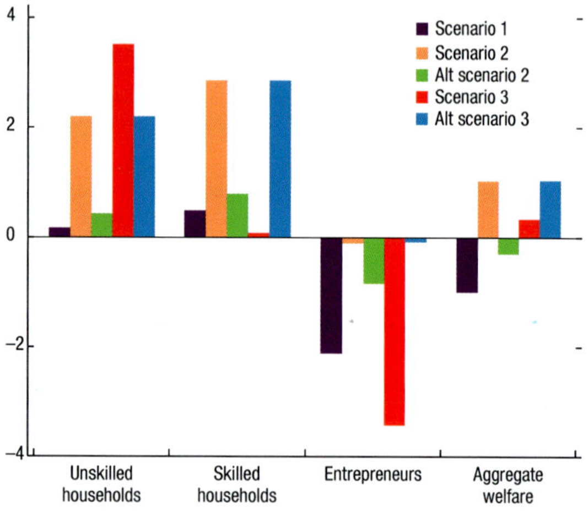

Source: IMF staff simulations.
Note: Welfare is measured as present discounted value of consumption utility.

level of effective consumption taxes needed to finance the increased government outlays (since taxes are distortionary); and (3) the price of energy (since energy is an intermediate input for production and its price impacts the profitability of the business sector). Overall, Scenario 2 has a powerful general equilibrium effect on capital returns and capital-intensive industries; higher private investment and lower rationing more than compensate for the negative effects of higher taxes required to finance the subsidy. In consequence, GDP increases significantly.[10] Scenario 1 has a negative effect on GDP (by 0.5 percent relative to baseline) because the reduction in rationing is not sufficient to compensate for the effects of higher taxes needed to pay for energy imports.[11] Scenario 3 displays the strongest reduction in GDP. This happens because energy is an input in production and higher energy prices increase production costs. Higher costs result in lower profitability (more so in sectors that are more energy intensive), with negative effects on overall economic performance. If the TFP of the energy sector increases by at least 12 percent, as discussed in the previous paragraph, then the impact of GDP in modified Scenario 3 could be as high as in Scenario 2.

Turning to distributional and welfare consequences, households benefit across the different scenarios, while entrepreneurs incur modest losses (Figure 43). For households, the reduction in rationing is more beneficial to them (in terms of welfare) than the cost of higher consumption taxes. Hence, households' welfare increases in all scenarios relative to the baseline. Because

[10]The model does not consider the possibility that subsidies could have adverse long-term effects (for instance, if subsidies were to reduce incentives and capacity to invest). If these effects were incorporated, this could reduce the benefits of Scenario 2.

[11]The main analysis abstracts from reforms that may improve SOE productivity under Scenario 1. Alternative simulations (not shown in the figures) find that an increase of 12 percent in the TFP of the SOE-producing energy would be necessary for Scenario 1 to match the energy increases attained by Scenario 2. In this case, real GDP would be broadly similar to the baseline, and still be 0.17 percent below Scenario 2. The reason the output outcome is still lower than under Scenario 2, despite the higher TFP, is because the investment subsidy of Scenario 2 increases private investment a bit more in all sectors of activity, compared to Scenario 1 (with higher TFP), which primarily affects investment in the energy sector but minimally elsewhere.

Figure 44. Gini Coefficient
(Difference between Scenario Gini and Baseline Gini coefficients)

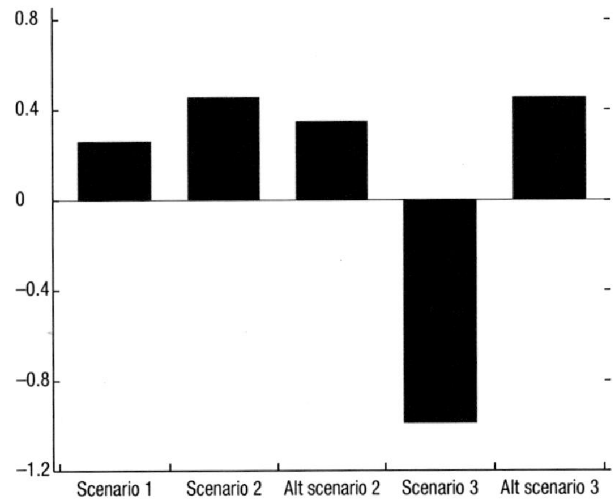

Source: IMF staff simulations.

high-skill individuals are assumed to face more energy rationing in the baseline (due to the nature of their economic activities and their consumption basket), they are also the ones that benefit the most in Scenario 2. Unskilled households benefit as well in this scenario because of the trickle-down effects of improved economic activity on their income.[12] In Scenario 1, households do not gain much relative to the baseline because taxes also increase and they still face significant rationing. In Scenario 3, higher-income individuals do not gain as much as in the other scenarios, because they consume more energy in the baseline and face higher energy costs. In addition, their incomes rely more on capital, and capital profitability falls with increasing energy costs. In Scenario 3, lower-income, unskilled households receive cash transfers and more energy is available, so they end up with substantial gains (without cash transfers they would have experienced substantial losses). Regarding entrepreneurs, they experience losses in welfare in all scenarios (relative to the baseline) because higher labor costs due to higher labor demand lower their profit. The mechanisms described so far help understand the impact on the net income Gini (namely, after government transfers and taxes) across alternative scenarios (Figure 44). Scenarios 1 and 2 result in higher overall Gini and household Gini, since higher consumption taxes are regressive and lower-income households consume little energy. Scenario 3 has a lower Gini because of the targeted cash transfers. Not all households benefit equally from changes in productivity (which benefit mostly energy-intensive sectors); this is why inequality goes up in modified Scenario 3 with higher productivity.

Overall, the comparison of the scenarios highlights stylized conditions under which private provision can be beneficial as well as the possible costs and risks associated with this option:

[12]Note that this beneficial effect would quasi disappear in the modified version of Scenario 2, wherein productivity is assumed to be lower.

- No scenario dominates others in all circumstances and taking into account all indicators of performance (production of services, economic growth, distributional implications).
- Using public funds to incentivize private investment can improve the production of and access to infrastructure services when the cost of public production is relatively high and/or productivity is lower in the public than in the private sector. Under the current calibration of the model, the impact of public funds on energy supply is twice as high when these funds are used to support private provision rather than financing more public expenditure.
- From the macroeconomic perspective, the best option seems to be the "ideal" subsidy of Scenario 2. However, its superior properties rest on its "perfect" design, in the sense that this subsidy targets very precisely the market failure and the rationing problem by narrowing the gap between costs and returns. In practice, such "surgical" subsidy is very hard to implement, partly because of the difficulty of targeting it toward firms that really need it and for which production would become suddenly profitable after receiving the subsidy. In a more realistic scenario with a poorly targeted subsidy (going to firms that would have produced otherwise and leading to a general decline in productivity growth), Scenario 2 would become far less favorable.
- The analysis also highlights the general equilibrium effects of the deregulation approach (Scenario 3), in which the price hike could negatively affect growth and income distribution. For deregulation to dominate the public investment and subsidy scenarios, two critical conditions are necessary: (1) a considerable boost to efficiency linked to private sector participation and (2) recourse to targeted social transfers to protect the poor. None of these conditions is guaranteed without proper policy design.
- Finally, the model suggests that price deregulation can be beneficial when there is broadly a 20 percent productivity increase relative to a situation with inefficient subsidies. Based on the empirical literature, this order of magnitude seems within reach.

Practical Considerations: Design and Conditions for Public Incentives

General Considerations

This section focuses on the measures deployed in the context of market failures. There are two main ways of justifying government interventions with the private sector. The primary motivation of pro-business measures is to remove government-induced distortions—such as red tape, burdensome licensing requirements, or imperfect contract enforcement—which repress entrepreneurship. However, this approach may not suffice in the presence of market imperfections: private sector participation can remain limited, even when government-imposed barriers are, to a large extent, eliminated (see, for instance, Rodrik 2004). Therefore, when market failures block private investment and discourage private finance, a second and complementary approach is warranted. This second approach relies on the use of explicit government incentives, such as targeted tax breaks, provision of public infrastructure to crowd-in private activities, R&D patents, or tariffs to protect nascent industries (Cheriff and Hasanov 2019). The measures discussed in this section, such as PPPs and blending arrangements, fall into this second category. And the terms "government incentives" or "government support" are used in the rest of the paper to describe this type of measures.

Government incentives comprise various forms of guarantees and subsidies. Government incentives are used to boost the risk-adjusted returns of financial investors up to the point where the project's payoffs match the investors' expected returns given the level of risks and alternative investing opportunities. Although a large variety of government support measures exist to attract financing for private or semi-private projects, they generally fall into two main broad categories—either a government guarantee (to reduce perceived risks) or a subsidy (to improve returns). In the rest of the section, the term "subsidy" is used, loosely, to describe a range of transfers that benefit financial investors directly or indirectly, including outright subsidies going to the project or to the financier, tax breaks, in-kind grants, and capital contributions.[13]

An instrument widely used in the world to incentivize private investment and attract private finance is the PPP framework. PPPs occupy a middle ground between traditional public provision and full private provision. They refer to long-term arrangements under which the private sector supplies infrastructure assets and infrastructure-based services that have traditionally been provided by the government. Therefore, PPPs covers a wide spectrum of models such as concessions and design-build-finance-operate-transfer. The private sector provider is responsible for not just asset delivery, but the overall project management and implementation, successful operation for several years thereafter and, typically, project financing. A key difference between PPPs and traditional public procurement is that debt is partly or mostly incurred by the private sector under a standard PPP.[14] The private sector partner will recover the investment and financing costs by charging fees to customers (for example, tolls) or to the government (availability payments) or a combination (Box 7).

[13]See a typology of government incentives in Irwin (2003).

[14]Note that the debt incurred by the private sector can possibly be reclassified by statisticians as government debt if the PPP asset is considered as remaining public (see below).

Nonetheless, PPPs still represent a relatively small market in Africa. On average, less than 10 percent of infrastructure projects in SSA are conducted under PPPs, with annual investment flows representing about half a percent of GDP (World Bank 2017b). In addition, PPPs are concentrated in a few sectors—mostly energy and, to a smaller extent, transportation—and a few countries (Kenya, Nigeria, South Africa, and Uganda). The relatively limited use of PPPs in Africa is due to a number of factors, including the small size of African economies, still-weak legal and regulatory frameworks for procuring and implementing PPPs, high project costs, a poor track record of PPPs in terms of investment,[15] and conflicts and other forms of instability in several countries.

Efficient Design of Public Incentives

Certain design features can maximize the efficiency and impact of public incentives, while minimizing risks. Public support to the private sector should obey a number of general principles, although the specific design must, of course, be tailored to the context and instrument:[16]

- *Address a clear market failure.* Public support should be targeted and granted on the basis of proven market failures. Otherwise, subsidies are superfluous and possibly distortionary—for instance, when a subsidy provided to an otherwise worthwhile private project sets the benchmark expectations for similar projects and crowds out non-subsidized and unable-to-compete projects, eventually reducing the market size.
- *Preferably temporary.* In general, public support should be temporary, unless there is clear evidence that the identified market failures are not expected to dissipate over time. Risks are often more important in the initial phase of development of an infrastructure project or of a market. In this context, it may be legitimate for the government to incentivize first movers and help entice a commitment to a new and higher-risk market when investors are keen to learn about it and develop local understanding, capacity and expertise. For instance, incentives have been successfully used to foster the development of renewable energy in some developing countries before production costs went down (World Bank 2018a). However, a private project (or a market segment) that needs permanent subsidies to survive

[15]Leigland (2018) reviews the experience of PPPs in developing countries and finds no clear evidence that investment (in terms of capacity building) increases with private participation—compared to non-PPP projects—despite the existence of efficiency gains.

[16]See, for instance, Irwin (2003) on the pros and cons of various forms of government support to private infrastructure; IMF (2015a) on tax incentives for investment; or Sulser (2018) on incentives for equity and debt investors in the context of infrastructure PPPs in developing countries.

is likely to be nonviable and, in this case, should not be incentivized by the government.

- *Display additionality.* Public incentives are meant to make worthy projects happen that would not happen otherwise. Thus, public support should display a "leverage" or "multiplier" effect, meaning that the catalyzed private investment should be additional, not only to the public contribution, but also to the investment that the private sector would have made otherwise without support. There is no additionality if a project had happened anyway, without subsidy, at broadly similar size and quality. From the government perspective, additionality also requires that the public incentive leads to higher and better services than if the government had done the project in a more traditional way without involving the private sector. In practice, additionality is very difficult to prove, in part because of the need to establish counterfactuals. But international institutions focused on private sector operations have developed frameworks to measure it (see, for instance, EBRD 2018).[17] One criterion to demonstrate additionality is to document the existence of market failures. Another approach taken in the context of PPPs is to assess the "value for money" of a project by comparing the net costs for the government under the PPP and traditional public procurement. One condition to observe a leverage effect is having positive value for money; otherwise the government should carry out the project in its budget and keep it on its balance sheet.
- *Leave sufficient risk and control with the private sector.* The allocation of risk is a fundamental question, not only to ensure that the efficiency gains from private ventures materialize but also because an insufficient transfer of risks could lead statisticians to reclassify the liabilities of the private party as public debt, which can be problematic for countries in which government debt is already very high.[18] Importantly, the objective is not to transfer all risks to the private sector, but to distribute them in the most efficient way. In general, specific risks should go to the party best able to (1) influence the likelihood of the risk (for example, completion risk going to the agent in charge of construction); (2) anticipate or respond to the risk factor (for example, shifting inflation risk to users by linking tariffs to CPI); and (3)

[17]An IEG desk review of the IFC activities during 1996–2007 suggested that IFC involvement was essential for the project to go ahead in only 27 percent of cases (IEG 2008). And in an additional 53 percent of cases, the IFC was at least "catalytic."

[18]Under accrual accounting (Government Finance Statistics Manual—GFSM and International Public Sector Accounting Standards—IPSAS), the debt incurred by the private sector may be reclassified as government debt if the asset of the PPP is assessed by statisticians as being public (even it is legally owned by the private sector). The criterion under IPSAS is whether the government controls de facto the asset (that is, controls the services provided and owns the asset at the end of the contract). For GFSM, the criterion is whether the government bears most of the project's risks and rewards.

absorb the risk (for example, tariff setting could be left to public sector) (OECD 2008).

- *Minimize the risk of contingent liabilities for the state.* Any form of public support is likely to create implicit or explicit contingent liabilities for the government, at least because it creates expectations with private investors that the government may provide further support along the way if the project fails. A proper design of the PPPs contracts and laws can, to some extent, minimize these risks (see Irwin, Mazraani, and Saxena 2018). The IMF and the World Bank have also developed an analytical tool called PPP Fiscal Risk Assessment Model (PFRAM), which helps assess potential fiscal costs and risks arising from PPP projects (IMF and World Bank 2019).

Subsidies or Guarantees?

In theory, various forms of government incentives could achieve broadly similar results when properly calibrated and designed. As discussed above, a wide range of measures are available to promote private sector activity and attract financing toward viable projects. All these measures can alter incentives and improve the risk-adjusted returns of financial investors—either by raising returns or reducing risks. Conceptually, the investor's return is the discounted factor equating the net present value of an asset's payoffs with its purchase price. If the states of the world and associated probabilities were known, it would be possible to (1) precisely calibrate the level of government support needed to achieve the investor's hurdle rate and (2) achieve the same increase in return through a subsidy or a guarantee.[19] Although these equivalences seem theoretical, the calibration of government support—for instance, in the context of PPPs—relies often on simple mathematical models.

In practice, subsidies present some advantages over guarantees in terms of transparency, fiscal risks, and moral hazard.[20] First, subsidies are generally more transparent. Their cost and beneficiaries are budgeted and known. In contrast, guarantees are subject to less budget scrutiny and monitoring. They can be used to hide fiscal costs, bypass expenditure controls, and subsidize projects and beneficiaries that the government favors in a nontransparent way, which poses governance problems. Second, guarantees introduce a degree of uncertainty in the management of the budget given their contingent nature.

[19]Assuming two states of the world (one with default with probability p, and the other one without default with probability 1–p), a subsidy S (paid in both states of the world), a guarantee G (paid in the state of the world with default and probability p), a payoff of 1 in the state of the world without default, and a one-period asset, then $p.S/(1+i)+(1-p).(1+S)/(1+i)=p.G(1+i)+(1-p)/(1+i)$. Then: $G= S/p$. In addition, the level of subsidy necessary to raise the return from i (without subsidy) to the hurdle rate i' (including subsidy) is: $S=[(1-p).i'-i]/(1+i)$.

[20]An advantage of guarantees over subsidies is that the latter can entail high transaction costs when there are multiple beneficiaries.

Although several analytical methods exist to value guarantees and predict their likely impact on the budget, the exercise is by nature very complex and imprecise, since risks can rarely be fully quantified and it may be impossible to estimate precisely the impact of the scheme in all states of the world (Hemming 2006; Razlog, Marrison, and Irwin 2020). Thus, government guarantees tend to create more fiscal risks than subsidies, as illustrated by the high costs of guarantees that are called (see estimates in Bova and others 2016). Third, even if subsidies are not immune to moral hazard, guarantees create serious incentive problems when the investor benefiting from the guarantee can, to some extent, influence its triggers. At the extreme, guarantees can create a culture where the private sector does not manage risks anymore. Nonetheless, a sound and well-thought-out design of guarantees can contain moral hazard by (1) limiting their use to risks that are outside the control of the private sector and cannot be diversified away or insured against, and (2) minimizing adverse incentive effects through, for instance, deductibles, collateral requirements, or risk-based fees (Hemming 2006, Saxena 2017).

The Question of the Cost

A fundamental issue is presented by the challenge of properly calibrating the value and number of public incentives to attract financial investors without overcompensating them. In theoretical models with market failures, it is generally recommended that the subsidy be equal to the value of the externality, but this criterion does not provide much practical guidance. Although competitive bidding for PPP contracts can, to some extent, mitigate the risk of miscalibration, the exercise remains complicated, highly technical, and uncertain, relying on many assumptions. For instance, USDT (2016) provides guidance on how to perform this calibration for highways PPPs to compensate fairly both bondholders and equity holders that have different requirements in terms of expected returns and the financing structure of the project. Difficulties in assessing the adequate level of government support and involvement are even more acute in low-income countries, wherein civil servants have typically less expertise and capacity to negotiate, assess, and monitor complex contracts and arrangements compared to private parties; this may result in excessive and uneven costs and risks being transferred to the public sector.

Experience with PPPs in developing countries shows that attracting the private sector requires the government to have skin in the game. When governments contemplate possible PPPs, they often have in mind an idealized (and unrealistic) model in which PPPs would be "self-sustained," meaning that (1) upfront costs to build assets would be entirely financed by private debt and private equity, (2) revenues during the operation phase would be gen-

Figure 45. Sources of PPP Financing in SSA, 2011–20

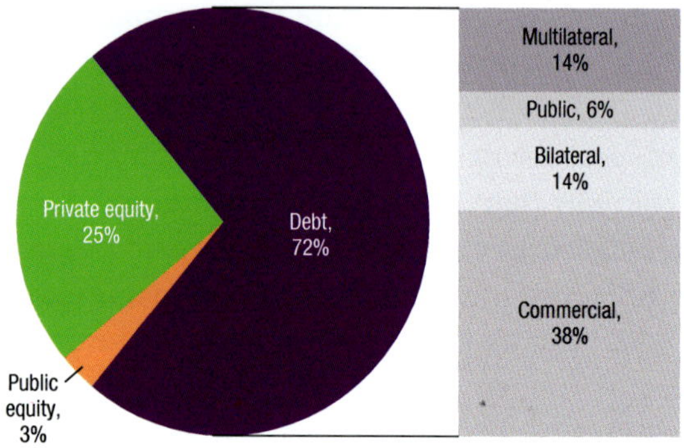

Sources: World Bank; Private Participation in Infrastructure Database; and IMF staff calculations.

erated solely from service sales (without much contributions from the government), and (3) most risks and costs would be borne by the private sector. In practice, PPPs in Africa depart significantly from this fictitious model (World Bank 2017b). This is particularly visible in the composition of financing. For instance, public money—both from national governments and DFIs—financed on average nearly 40 percent of PPP projects' investment costs in SSA during 2011–20 (Figure 45). As a result, PPPs in Africa have been closer to cofinancing schemes than to "pure" private projects, which is also the case more generally in developing countries.[21]

Government incentives are often needed to ensure the financial viability of development projects.[22] Estache and Philippe (2012) review two decades of private sector participation in infrastructure in developing countries. They find that sectors such as telecommunications and electricity generation, in which cost-reflective tariffs seem less controversial, have proven to be reasonably profitable and largely free of subsidies. But most other sectors in low-income countries—electricity distribution and transmission, transport, and water and sanitation—tend to require government support to sustain cash flows and bring the rate of return close to the cost of capital. This finding is confirmed by the World Bank PPI database, which shows that two-thirds of the PPI deals in low- and middle-income countries had received some form of direct or indirect government support during 2011–20. And this share does not even include the incentives possibly provided by international institutions, which are another form of public support.[23]

In the case of SSA projects, government subsidies seem to be less common than guarantees. In SSA, about half of the projects have received some form

[21]Other studies using the PPI data set with a broader country sample find similar results. For instance, World Bank (2018c) shows that, in International Development Association countries, public sources financed 45 percent of PPI projects in 2017. Using an even broader data set (all low- and middle-income countries), World Bank (2020a) finds a share of close to 40 percent in 2019.

[22]While the previous paragraph analyzes the financing structure of projects, the next paragraphs focus on government incentives, which take the form of *direct support* (payments from the budget, including capital subsidy during the project construction phase or revenue subsidy, like availability payment, provided during the operational phase) and *indirect support* (for example, various forms of guarantees and tax breaks).

[23]World Bank (2020a) finds that only 5 percent of PPI projects in developing countries had benefited from a guarantee from DFIs in 2019. Thus, the size of the incentives provided by DFIs should not be overstated.

Table 5. Government Support to PPI Infrastructure Projects
Projects 2011–20

Region	No Support	Direct Support Only	Indirect Support Only	Both Direct and Indirect Support	Total Projects	Projects Receiving Support
	(Number of Projects)					(Percent of Total)
East Asia and Pacific	67	430	200	8	705	90.5
Europe and Central Asia	88	49	91	2	230	61.7
Latin America and the Caribbean	305	65	199	0	569	46.4
Middle East and North Africa	12	9	45	0	66	81.8
South Asia	253	210	128	3	594	57.4
Sub-Saharan Africa	67	10	50	1	128	47.7
Memorandum items:						
Non-Sub-Saharan Africa	725	763	663	13	2,164	66.5
All Regions	792	773	713	14	2,292	65.4

Sources: PPI database, World Bank; and IMF staff calculations.
Note: Only projects with available data on the existence or absence of government support have been included.

of direct or indirect government support during 2011–20.[24] This share is lower than in the rest of low- and middle-income countries (Table 5). When it comes to *direct support*, less than 10 percent of PPP infrastructure projects in SSA rely significantly on annuity/availability payments or other forms of subsidies from the government in their revenue structure.[25] This is partly because PPPs in the region have historically been concentrated in the energy sector, which collects revenue through power purchase agreements (World Bank 2017b). In this regard, SSA countries differ from other developing countries where direct support from the government is more common, especially in the water sector (World Bank 2016).[26] On the other hand, *indirect support* appears to be more prevalent in SSA. For instance, 40 percent of the SSA projects during 2011–20 had received indirect support, mostly in the form of payment guarantees, which are typical of energy projects.

Costs for the government may not materialize upfront. This is what the past experience of PPPs in developing countries shows (see reviews in Harris 2003, Estache and Philippe 2012, Leigland 2018). It is common for the project preparation stage to underestimate the costs and support needed from the government, while overestimating the gains and profitability for the private operator, for instance, by overestimating expected demand. This bias is partly due to the absence of thorough and systematic value-for-money and

[24]This share is based on the analysis of PPI deals during 2011–20: 61 deals received either direct or indirect support or both, out of the 128 deals for which information on public support is available (Table 5).

[25]The World Bank PPI database distinguishes three sources of revenue for a project: (1) user fees, (2) power or water purchase agreements and sales to wholesale markets, and (3) annuity/availability paid by the government.

[26]In non-SSA countries during 2011–20, about 30 percent of the infrastructure projects had received indirect support (mostly payment guarantees but also revenue guarantees and tariff rate guarantees), while one-third of the projects had received direct support (mostly revenue subsidy and capital subsidy) according to the World Bank PPI database (Table 5).

cost-benefit analyses, but also to distorted incentives from both the government and private sector. For instance, governments may be attracted to PPPs because they see them as a way of shifting project costs off their books. And private investors may underbid to win a contract, under the assumption that they can negotiate better terms later. As a result, many PPP contracts are often initially unprofitable for the private sector, especially in the first decade, and are subsequently renegotiated, resulting in high ex post costs for the government.

In addition, there are indirect costs associated with compensating the losers of private sector participation reforms. The review studies cited in the previous paragraph show that PPPs and other forms of private participation in infrastructure do generate efficiency gains, but they are not necessarily equally distributed among stakeholders. For instance, employment often declines with private participation—reflecting the fact that inefficient SOEs were often overstaffed and reforms lead to redundancies. In addition, tariffs are sometimes increased where they were previously far below cost-recovery, and this practice negatively affects poor households, which face higher purchase price for services or can even lose access. This means that the government may need to compensate or support some parts of the population.[27] For instance, targeted cash transfers to the poor have long been recommended as a key component of reform packages introducing cost-recovery tariffs and eliminating fuel subsidies in the energy sector (Coady and others 2015).

Innovative Ways of Providing Incentives: The Example of Blending

In a world in which government resources are increasingly scarce and fiscal space is limited, SSA countries may not be able or willing to support the budgetary cost of incentives necessary to attract private finance. As discussed in the previous section, there are ways to make government incentives more efficient. But no matter how well designed these incentives could be, they will remain costly. If direct and indirect costs are too high for government budgets, a solution could be to shift (part of) them to third parties, such as donors or philanthropic institutions.

An often-discussed proposal for fostering private investment without straining governments' budgets is the blending model. Blending is a framework in which concessional financing[28] from donors is used, along with public commercial finance (for example, standard DFI operations), to catalyze

[27]For a discussion on the budgetary costs associated with facilitating and incentivizing structural reforms, see Banerji and others (2017).

[28]Concessional financing denotes loans extended on terms more generous than the market as well as pure grants.

private commercial finance. Strictly speaking, blending requires the three components (concessional financing, public commercial finance, and private commercial finance), although there are less restrictive definitions.[29] Conceptually, blending differs both from standard DFI operations and the PPP framework, which in principle do not rely so explicitly and systematically on concessional financing—although DFI operations generally provide lending at sub-commercial terms and most PPPs deviate from the optimal model of "self-sustained" PPP financed by user fees and rely on some form of public subsidies. The blending paradigm features a more explicit recognition that some projects may be profitable for the private sector only if they receive a form of subsidy, which will result in outright "losses" for donors (Box 8).

A greater role of the donor community in promoting private projects can also reduce the political risks perceived by the private sector. The role of DFIs and donors goes, indeed, beyond sharing risk and alleviating the financial constraints of the private sector. Their involvement as co-investor in projects is also highly valued by private investors, who anticipate that the government partner is more likely to maintain some stability in the business environment and honor the terms of joint public-private contracts. Large development institutions, especially multilateral ones, may have some traction on national authorities given the size of their lending portfolio and long-term working relationships. Therefore, even without explicit political risk guarantee, DFI participation may greatly reduce the counterparty risk perceived by private investors.

So far, blending has been relatively limited and fragmented. In 2019, private investment mobilized in low- and middle-income countries through blending was estimated in a range of $3–27 billion, compared to about $150 billion of ODA from the members of the OECD Development Assistance Committee, and tiny compared to the SDG financing gap (Attridge and Engen 2019). Most of the private finance mobilized through blending is concentrated in middle-income countries, with less than $2 billion annually going to low-income countries. Anecdotal evidence also suggests that blending facilities can be complex and nontransparent; African authorities and international investors are often unaware of the available instruments (Juvonen and others 2019).

And, like PPPs, blending is not cheap. Experience with blending facilities in low-income countries suggests that the degree of additionality is relatively

[29]Under the OECD definition, the condition that characterizes a blending arrangement is to have "development finance," which includes public commercial finance (from DFIs). Concessional financing is not necessary per se. Therefore, a scheme combining both public and private commercial finance would qualify as blending, according to the OECD.

low. Empirical analyses find that leverage ratios[30] are generally below 1, especially in the poorest countries.[31] This means that one dollar of public funds catalyzes less than one dollar of private funds. On average, leverage ratios are still positive, meaning that donor resources are not wasted compared to traditional budget support. However, they are far too low to catalyze the trillions of dollars necessary to close the infrastructure gap in Africa. And some projects do not show clear additionality, meaning that these projects would have happened without the subsidy (IEG 2008). Thus, large amounts of concessional finance are needed to have a material impact on private investment in development sectors. "Billions-to-billions" is more plausible than "billions to trillions."

Expanding greatly the scale of the blending model will be challenging. At least two bottlenecks need to be addressed (Kapoor 2019). The first one is the transparency risk. The provision and calibration of subsidies is made more opaque by the fact that private investors can use multiple blending facilities, whose number has grown significantly in recent years, and that these facilities entail complex procedures. Second, blending facilities are rarely run by private sector specialists with expertise in assessing and managing projects. Therefore, blending is not always granted on the basis of proven market failures and can be distortionary and squeeze out nonsubsidized projects.

Overall, a large scaling-up of blending would require a rethink of its governance structure to achieve better coordination, consolidation, and greater transparency of facilities. DFIs, which have the expertise, mandate, and financial capacity for fostering private sector development, could play a central role in this effort, by coordinating and enhancing the dialogue among governments, donors, and private sector investors. For instance, DFIs could help national authorities identify sectors and structural projects with the highest growth potential and impact. DFIs could directly receive donors' funds through special subsidy windows—similar to the IDA private sector window of the World Bank. Alternatively, donors could finance upstream activities, such as technical assistance for project development, which would indirectly benefit DFI operations.

[30]The literature has no single definition of the concept of "leverage ratio" on blending. Existing studies use multiple definitions. In this section, the authors characterize the leverage ratio of blending as the ratio of private commercial finance divided by public finance—both commercial and concessional.

[31]See review of estimates of leverage ratios in Attridge and Engen (2019).

Box 7. What Makes PPP Ventures Attractive to the Private Sector?

Although not their only objective, PPPs are a way to make projects available to and economically viable for the private sector. Several PPP features can attract private partners:

- PPPs allow the private sector to produce and sell services in areas that would otherwise be subject to entry barriers due to legal or social impediments (for example, the legislation may prevent the private sector from entering some activities such as water distribution, or there may be strong sentiments against privatization of such services).
- Infrastructure assets under PPPs often have a monopoly or an oligopolistic position in a market, with demand behavior being inelastic to the economic cycle (O'Neill 2009). The privileged position of the infrastructure operator is commonly guaranteed by legislation or through the compliance of an industry regulator or even through direct earnings assurances.
- PPPs generally allow private partners to collect and possibly increase user fees, including in sectors where there was no culture for paying for these services.
- The government often provides financial support to make PPPs attractive to private partners. During the construction phase, the government can inject equity or debt in the SPV, or grant a subsidy (or, equivalently, a tax break). It can also guarantee the SPV debt. Often, the government also conducts complementary public works (for example, utilities). During the operation phase, if the PPP is government funded, the government makes an annual/monthly payment for services to the private operator ("availability payments"). It may also guarantee a minimum revenue.
- PPP contracts typically span a few decades to guarantee a sufficient stream of revenue that will compensate the private partner for the investment made. For instance, infrastructure projects can generate predictable, stable, and often inflation-adjusted returns over long periods of time.
- PPPs entail an allocation and transfer of risks, which may suit the private sector, with the government keeping the risks that the former cannot control or affect, such as regulatory and political risks. The government could, for instance, keep the demand risk when the private sector cannot affect the demand level, such as in the prison or education sectors.

Box 8. Examples of Blending Instruments

Blending uses international grants or other concessional resources to enhance the returns and/or reduce the risks of private projects:

- *Direct grants.* Grants are provided by the donor either directly to the project or to the lender to allow for better financing conditions.[1] Grants can be conditional and performance-based; for instance, the donor agrees to pay off the debt of the project upon successful achievement of predetermined performance indicators.
- *Guarantees.* Guarantees cover a portion of private loan or bond repayments. They are provided by donors to lenders to cover commercial or noncommercial risks (for example, expropriation, currency transfer restriction and inconvertibility, war, and civil disturbance . . .). For instance, some guarantee products enhance the terms of commercial debt by covering the payment of principal and/or interest up to a predetermined amount. This improves the conditions of and access to financing for the project.
- *Credit tranching and bundling.* Project financing instruments may be sliced into tranches to match the different appetite for risk of different financial investors. Donors can invest in the highest risk tranche of the project shielding other investors from a predefined amount of financial losses ("first-loss provisions"). Furthermore, multiple projects can be re-bundled into a portfolio that aims at mitigating risk for financial investors with a lower risk appetite, such as pension funds.
- *Risk capital.* Donors can make equity investments in high-risk projects. This creates incentives for other investors, because equity is the riskiest part of the balance sheet.
- *FX hedging mechanisms.* These schemes provide cost-effective solutions in countries that have no widespread hedging mechanisms. For instance, when local investors borrow in foreign currency and use the cash generated by the project (in local currency) to repay the foreign exchange loan, the currency risk can be reduced or even eliminated through hedging instruments that swap the foreign exchange debt obligations into local currency obligations.
- *Technical assistance.* Donor-financed capacity development can strengthen project preparation and implementation, reducing future risks.

[1]For instance, a grant can be provided to pay for specific goods linked to the project (the individuals or firms use the grant to replace or upgrade some fixed assets); as a result, they do not need to borrow as much, which reduces their financing cost. Or the grant can be provided directly to the bank to lower the interest rate on the loan ("interest-rate subsidy"); thus, the project will receive a subsidized loan at below-market interest rate.

CHAPTER

6 Finding New Sources of Private Finance

There are several large, and mostly unrealized, sources of private finance, which African countries could tap into in the medium term. Recently, some discussion has focused on the possibility of mobilizing the vast resources of foreign institutional investors and philanthropists to finance development projects in Africa. This section shows that a large potential exists but it is by no means low-hanging fruit, because institutional investors tend to be risk-adverse and constrained by domestic regulations, while philanthropists do not have the vehicles and channels of implementation to invest in a large scale in the poorest and most fragile economies, especially outside the health sector.

Institutional Investors

Global institutional investors encompass a heterogenous group of investors that seek to maximize financial returns on their assets. Institutional investors are entities that invest in different asset classes and pool risks on behalf of their members, while being bound to meet a minimum threshold of financial return. They include insurance companies, pension funds, mutual funds, and sovereign wealth funds among others (Box 9). Many of these investors, such as pension funds and insurance companies, tend to have a longer-term investment outlook to match the maturity of their liabilities. At the global level, the role of institutional investors as providers of long-term finance has increased in the past decade as a result of tighter regulations on banks (OECD 2016). Like the rest of the paper, this chapter focuses mostly on international investors, although there is a growing domestic base of African institutional investors, for which many recommendations of this chapter are also relevant.

Figure 46. Assets Under the Management of OECD Institutional Investors, 2005–19

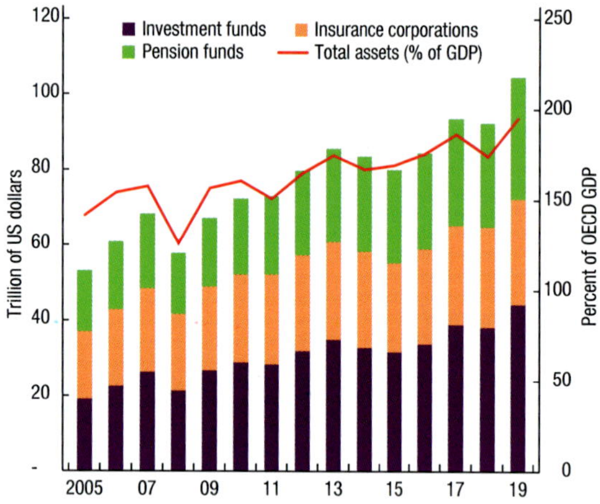

Source: OECD Institutional Investors Statistics 2020.

Size and Scope of the Investor Base

Institutional investors in the OECD manage large resources of about $100 trillion. At the end of 2019, assets under management of institutional investors in OECD countries were estimated at $105 trillion (OECD 2020a).[1] Investment funds[2] were the largest investor (accounting for more than 40 percent of all assets at the end of 2019), followed by pension funds (30 percent) and insurance companies (about a quarter). Combined assets of these investors nearly doubled on average between 2005 and 2019, with the largest growth observed in assets managed by investment funds (Figure 46).

Allocations of institutional investors in African infrastructure remain very limited. Because no consolidated data on investment allocations by region and type of assets is available, this section relies on information from various surveys. In some cases, information is available only for a category of institutional investors or for a single year. The main findings are as follows:

- Regarding the *regional allocation* of institutional investors, OECD (2017a) shows that pensions funds invested about 90 percent of their funds in AEs in 2016. And Africa accounted for a meager half a percent of total foreign investments of the pension funds that were surveyed (Figure 47).
- Regarding the *type of assets*, Preqin (2020a) reports that institutional investors, like pension funds and insurance companies, typically commit only 2–3 percent of their total assets to infrastructure, while sovereign wealth funds and superannuation schemes have larger allocations of 5–6 percent (Figure 48). Focusing on a sample of large pension funds and public pen-

[1]The majority of institutional investors are concentrated in OECD countries. Data on institutional investors from other regions are scarce but likely to be small compared to OECD figures. For instance, assets of non-OECD pension funds were estimated at about $734 billion at the end of 2019, which is about 2 percent of assets of pension funds in the OECD (OECD 2020a).

[2]In the OECD database on institutional investors, "investment funds" are defined as institutional units that consolidate investor funds for the purpose of acquiring financial assets. Examples are mutual funds, investment trusts, unit trusts, and other collective investment units.

Figure 47. Allocation of Overseas Investments of Selected Pension Funds, 2016
(Percent of total foreign investment)

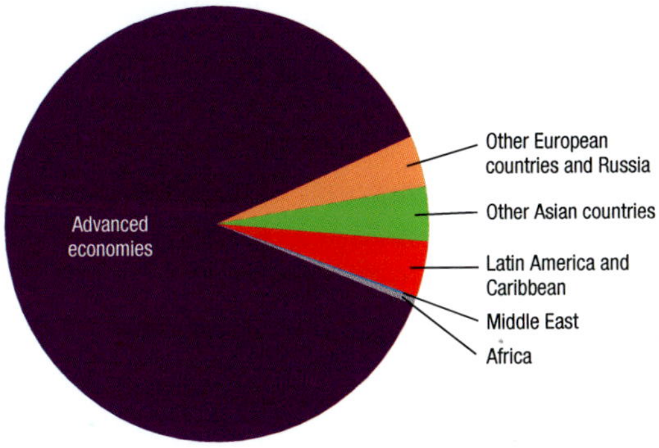

Source: Authors' calculations based on OECD (2017a).
Note: Based on a sub-sample of pensions funds in 25 countries for which data are available.

Figure 48. Investors' Median Current Allocations to Infrastructure by Investor Type, 2019
(Percent of assets under management)

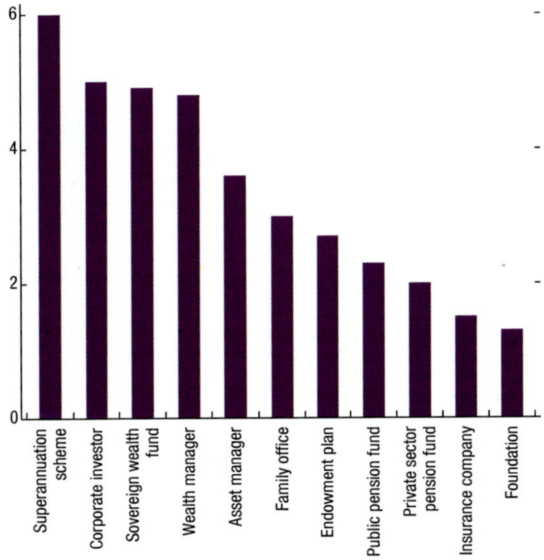

Source: Preqin (2020)

sion reserve funds, OECD (2019b) finds that they allocated, on average, 1.3 percent of total assets to infrastructure in the form of unlisted equity and debt. World Bank (2018a), which reviews infrastructure projects in developing countries, finds that institutional investors contributions to PPI investments amounted to only 0.67 percent of the total projects' size during 2011–17.

- *Combining these two dimensions*, investment in infrastructure in Africa is likely to be very small, although limited information is available. In the 2019 OECD survey of large pension funds, no pension funds reported exposure to infrastructure investments in Africa (OECD 2019b). Another perspective is given by the amounts raised by unlisted infrastructure funds in the region: only 24 Africa-focused infrastructure funds reached a final close between 2007 and 2016, raising cumulatively $4.6 billion from institutional investors (Preqin 2016).[3]

Nonetheless, institutional investors' appetite for infrastructure is growing. OECD pension funds tend to allocate the largest share of their portfolios (60 percent) into traditional assets such as equity, bills and bonds, and cash and deposits (Figure 49). Yet the composition of portfolios has increasingly shifted toward alternative asset classes, such as unlisted private equity,

[3]However, global funds with an investment remit that includes Africa are much larger. Over the same period, 115 global vehicles reached a final close, securing $102 billion in capital commitments.

Figure 49. Asset Allocation of OECD Pension Funds across Different Assets, 2001–19
(Percent of total assets)

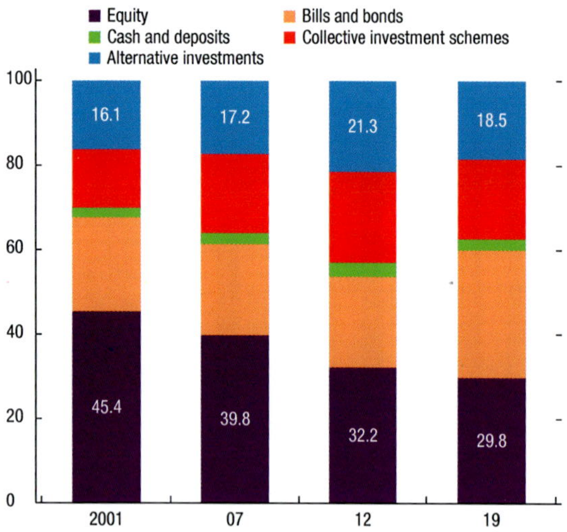

Source: OECD Global Pension Statistics Database.

unlisted infrastructure equity, lands, and buildings among others, which accounted for about 19 percent of total investments at the end of 2019 (OECD 2020b). In addition, institutional investors see potential in Africa. A survey led by Preqin (2020b) shows that about 20 percent of these investors view Africa as presenting the best investment opportunities in infrastructure among all emerging markets.

Looking forward, a huge untapped potential exists for African countries. Allocations to infrastructure are below targets for many institutional investors. Focusing on pension funds, OECD (2019b) finds that target allocations among the funds with dedicated exposure to infrastructure assets ranged from 1 to up to 20 percent of total assets—well below actual allocations. Nearly all pension funds included in the survey reported that they were below targets at the end of 2017. And many funds that do not currently invest in infrastructure reported they were planning to open allocations in the future. A back-of-the envelope calculation gives a sense of the potential. If the share of Africa in the portfolio of institutional investors went from the current 0.5 percent to the weight of Africa in global GDP (about 2 percent), African assets under management would increase by $1,500 billion, equivalent to an annual flow of about $50 billion a year (over the lifetime of the infrastructure asset, assumed to be 30 years).

Attractiveness of Africa for Institutional Investors

In a global context of sustained low interest rates, infrastructure investments in Africa could offer relatively high, inflation-protected, and stable returns. First, the low-yield environment may prompt institutional investors to seek new forms investments to achieve their targeted return (IMF 2019c). Alternative assets such as infrastructure, which are riskier, less liquid, and less sought after, can potentially offer higher returns.[4] Also, prospects that SDG sectors are going to be growth engines in Africa over the next decade could

[4]See review of expected return differentials across asset classes in BFT BSDC (2018).

generate significant dividend expectations. A survey of international investors conducted in 2017 showed that a 6–7 percent premium was required for the return on equity of infrastructure investment in emerging markets relative to OECD countries (EDHEC 2017). In Africa, the targeted dollar return on infrastructure assets can be on the order of 20 percent (Mercer LLC 2018). Second, returns are often hedged against inflation, since user tariffs for infrastructure services are generally indexed (Deutsche Asset Management 2017). Third, returns can be relatively stable during the operation phase of the asset. This is because the demand for infrastructure assets tend to be relatively inelastic to the business cycle due to the essential nature of the services.

Infrastructure investments generate cash flows over long periods to time, matching the liability horizon of many institutional investors. Pension funds are bound by liability-driven investment strategies under which the objective is not simply to maximize returns for a given level of risk, but also to ensure that assets adequately provide for the institution's liabilities. SDG investments especially in infrastructure are typically made for the long term (for example, concessions of 25 years, leases up to 99 years) and thus seems a natural fit with the long-term liabilities of many pension funds. These assets offer institutional investors stable cash flows and income streams over a long period.

Infrastructure could also yield portfolio diversification benefits. Some claim that infrastructure assets have the potential to be a separate "asset class," enhancing portfolio diversification and expanding the risk-return frontier.[5] Nonetheless, the issue remains unsettled, with some evidence supporting the claim that unlisted infrastructure provides significant portfolio diversification benefits (Newel, Peng, and De Francesco 2011), while others find that the performance of listed infrastructure has a low correlation with other major assets (Blanc-Brude, Whittaker, and Wilde 2017).

Finally, SDG-related investment provides institutional investors with an opportunity to engage in impact-focused sectors. Beyond profitability and diversification benefits, investing in SDGs (especially in the social and environmental dimensions) can help cater for clients who demand both financial return and impact. The United Nations Principles for Responsible Investment were launched in 2006 to facilitate the incorporation by institutional investors of environmental, social, and governance issues into their investment decisions (PRI 2020a). The number of investor signatories has increased from 100 to 3,000, representing in 2020 more than $100 trillion of assets under management (PRI 2020b; Figure 50).

[5]A set of securities composes an "asset class" if their returns have high covariances (higher than with other assets). For that asset class to be appealing to investors it should expand the risk-return frontier—that is, adding infrastructure assets to a market portfolio that previously excluded them should either boost yields for the same level of risk or reduce risks for the same level of return.

Figure 50. Assets under Management in Responsible Investments, 2006–20

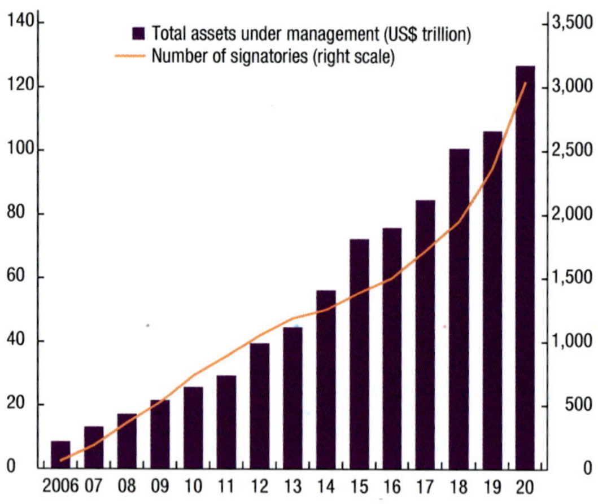

Source: PRI (2020b).

Bottlenecks to Further Involvement of Institutional Investors

Many SDG-related investments do not display the risk-return profile targeted by institutional investors. Two aspects are particularly problematic in this regard: the combination of high risks–low returns during the origination and construction phases, as well as the illiquidity of infrastructure assets, which makes divesture more difficult. Experience shows that, when they invest in infrastructure, institutional investors tend to favor brownfield projects, characterized by more stable revenue streams and a more predictable regulatory environment (World Bank 2018a).[6] But Africa's needs are mostly in greenfield projects, which require huge upfront investments and have long gestation periods before they can generate revenue streams in the operation phase (Juvonen and others 2019).

This issue is compounded by the relative scarcity of financial products tailored to infrastructure finance in SSA. Existing financing vehicles are often perceived as insufficiently developed and diversified to cater to the needs of various investors with different risk-return preferences as well as to modulate the financing options along the different stages of the project (design, construction, and operation).[7] In particular, the corporate equity and bond markets are narrow in most African countries, with debt instruments focusing on short-term maturities. Institutional investors can also provide funding through pooled investment vehicles, such as infrastructure funds that have become more widespread in Africa in recent years (Juvonen and others 2019). But Africa-focused investment funds remain a relatively small market segment (Preqin 2016), and fees can be relatively high for smaller institutional investors (OECD 2015). In addition, mismatches exist between the infrastructure asset life, which can be 20–30 years, and the investment horizon of collective investment vehicles, which is usually significantly shorter

[6]The exception is the energy sector in which institutional investors are more willing to invest in greenfield projects because the construction period is relatively short.

[7]For a typology of the vehicles available to institutional investors for infrastructure investment, see OECD (2014) and Inderst and Stewart (2014).

(for instance, five years for private equity funds and 10–15 years for infrastructure funds in Africa).

Direct investment in projects is particularly difficult.[8] Institutional investors often lack the technical and sector-specific expertise and experience to evaluate individual projects in Africa. Infrastructure projects entail unfamiliar legal and financial arrangements and carry idiosyncratic risks—for instance, construction risks when programs are delayed or costs are higher than budgeted, as well as operational, environmental, and regulatory risks (Inderst 2009). The lack of high-quality data on the performance of unlisted infrastructure assets compounds the difficulty of evaluating projects.

In addition, infrastructure assets remain a small market for international institutional investors, especially in Africa. There are at least two reasons for this. First, the lack of a pipeline of well-structured and viable infrastructure projects of sufficient size (discussed in Chapter 3) limits the visibility of existing opportunities and constrains the investors' engagement. It may also discourage institutional investors from expanding their technical capacity to assess projects in the region. Second, while infrastructure projects are by nature highly heterogeneous, available legal and financial products are not standardized, which segments an already-small market. This lack of standardization (in terms of documentation and contracts, financial products, adequate data, and benchmarks for measuring investment performance) increases transaction costs and risks for such investments. In this context, investors are not capable of comparing easily different investment opportunities, let alone scaling them up (Collier and Mayer 2014, World Bank 2018b).

Prudential regulations also limit the ability of institutional investors to hold lower-grade assets classes or invest abroad. Institutional investors must follow a number of national regulations, laws, and guidelines, with private equity firms and sovereign wealth funds being subject to fewer restrictions. This oversight is essential to mitigating financial stability risks and protecting the beneficiaries (for example, retirees or insured households), but it can create impediments to scaling up flows to African countries. There are four main bottlenecks:

- Regulatory requirements in the investor's country of origin restrict the institutional investors' *investment decisions*. In its annual survey of investment regulations of pension funds, OECD (2020c) shows, for instance, that, at the end of 2019, most pension funds were subject to investment

[8]In principle, institutional investors could invest either directly or indirectly in infrastructure projects in Africa: (1) they can purchase directly project bonds or general bonds as well as listed or unlisted equity issued by the project, or (2) they can invest indirectly through investment funds, such as private equity funds or pooled infrastructure funds.

limits both in terms of type of assets (especially for illiquid ones) and regional allocation (with some pension funds explicitly prohibited from investing outside the OECD).

- *Risk-based requirements* impose a higher capital charge for riskier investments of insurance companies, such as equity and low investment-grade debt, especially BBB-rated debt.[9] Solvency II, which is the European law that harmonizes the insurance regulation in Europe, may encourage insurers to seek shorter-term debt to meet regulatory solvency requirements (Kappel and Reisen 2017).
- *Accounting standards* can also constrain investment choices. In particular, the shift toward mark-to-market accounting may reduce incentives of institutional investors, such as pension funds, to hold illiquid infrastructure assets.
- Another potential constraint is the *rule adopted by rating agencies* for infrastructure projects in Africa (and many emerging market economies) that an African project cannot be rated higher than the sovereign debt of the country—a rule that is not applied in advanced economies (Collier 2014).

Unlocking Resources from Institutional Investors

Financial regulations that hinder the purchase of SDG-aligned assets in Africa could be harmonized and rethought. National regulations and international standards have been tightened in the aftermath of the global financial crisis to build a stronger safety net against financial risks. Without jeopardizing this broad objective of financial stability, regulatory authorities and the Financial Stability Board could initiate a dialogue on possible reforms of the rules or practices that create impediments to international investment in Africa. For instance, investment limits that apply to pension funds could be harmonized across countries, and some of the most restrictive rules could be relaxed, with a view to diversifying the pension funds' portfolios away from government securities and allowing them more systematically to invest abroad. In addition, risk-rating agencies could reconsider their practice of rating private projects in Africa systemically below sovereigns, since their respective debt-servicing capacities may be uncorrelated (for example, with a private company being able to service its debt in a country where the sovereign has defaulted) or even fundamentally different (since sovereign debt sustainability is constrained by low revenue mobilization and a high share of mandatory spending in Africa—two issues that are less relevant for private projects, where the revenue streams can be high and the execution of expenditure can be adjusted more flexibly in case of temporary difficulties to repay debt).

[9]Capital requirements do not apply to pension funds.

More standardization of contracts, products, and data would make infrastructure finance more attractive. Greater standardization of contracts and documentation in the various stages of an infrastructure project lifecycle (bidding, procurement) is critical to reducing their cost and complexity, as well as facilitating their comparability for investors (G20 2018). More standardized templates and checklists for structuring infrastructure projects would also encourage greater private sector participation. In addition, efforts could be made to build a transparent and comprehensive database on infrastructure projects and performance to help investors assess and compare investment opportunities. A successful one-time policy initiative has been the Africa Infrastructure Country Diagnostic, which collected a large amount of valuable information on infrastructure performance as well as detailed economic and technical data in 24 African countries during 2001–06 (Foster and Briceño-Garmendia 2010).

New or more-tailored financial products should be developed to better match the preferences of various institutional investors. The objective of these financing vehicles would be to diversify the supply of infrastructure-related financial products and make the risk-return profiles more palatable to investors. Although banks, DFIs, and governments are likely to remain key financiers in the early stages of new projects, they are not necessarily well placed to hold long-term assets on their balance sheets and/or do not always have the financial capacity to scale up projects. Unbundling the financing of infrastructure projects along the project lifecycle is, therefore, key to attracting new investors (Collier and Mayer 2014, Collier and others 2014, OECD 2015). In this regard, project bonds[10] could be appealing to large institutional investors, with their desirable features of tradability and liquidity (Ehlers 2014). The project bond market is still in the early stage of development in Africa, with the first listing and investment-grade infrastructure bond entirely held by institutional investors being issued in 2013 in South Africa (Deloitte 2014, OECD 2015). Other new forms of finance, such as infrastructure investment funds, could also help tap some of the vast resources of international capital markets. These funds could be specialized according to the development stage of the projects they invest in, since risks change considerably over the lifetime of a project; this would create efficiency gains and help offer a wider range of investment options to investors with different risk appetites. Finally, the securitization of bank infrastructure loans could also be a driving force. Through credit enhancement (tranching), various assets could meet the credit and liquidity requirements of institutional investors with different degrees of risk aversion (Ehlers 2014).

[10]Project bonds are bonds that are issued on the capital market to finance (or refinance) an infrastructure project and that are paid back exclusively from the flows of revenues generates by the project.

A larger pipeline of bankable infrastructure projects is an essential condition to giving visibility to the African market and prompting institutional investors to develop specialized capacity in evaluating projects. With the support of international institutions and donors, African authorities need to lay out national, long-term strategies for the infrastructure sector that last beyond the political cycle (OECD 2015). These strategies would identify and develop key projects to ensure a steady flow of well-developed and bankable investments opportunities. This issue is discussed more extensively in Chapter 4. While the importance of a sizeable project pipeline is relevant for all types of investors, it seems even more critical for institutional investors whose preferences are strongly oriented toward established and more mature projects.

Finally, the fact that a majority of institutional investors are relatively risk averse raises the question as to whether some public support could be needed to attract them. Experience shows that international investors are less averse to investing in speculative-grade countries if there is adequate multilateral, bilateral, or government support (Juvonen and others 2019). Reviewing a decade of infrastructure investments in developing countries, World Bank (2018a) shows that two-thirds of the projects with institutional investor contributions had required some government or DFI incentives. For example, the development of the renewable energy sector in South Africa has been propelled by payment guarantees provided by the government to institutional investors. The country was able to attract the highest level of institutional-investor investment (albeit local) through a programmatic approach launched in 2011 called the Renewable Energy Independent Power Producers Procurement Program.

Foundations and High-Wealth Philanthropic Individuals

Private philanthropic finance comprises private capital given through foundations and private wealth individuals. No strict definition of philanthropy exists.[11] Foundations are nongovernmental nonprofit organizations; their income, which is spent for socially useful purposes, is typically sourced from endowment, donations from companies and individuals, royalties, or lotteries. Global high-net-worth individuals (HNWI) are generally defined as persons or families that have investable financial assets of more than $1 mil-

[11]In the context of its recent data collection project, OECD (2018) defines "private philanthropy for development" as transactions from the private sector that have the promotion of the economic development and welfare of developing countries as their main objective and that originate from foundations' own sources, notably endowment, donations from companies and individuals (including HNWIs and crowdfunding), legacies, as well as income from royalties, investments (including government securities), dividends, lotteries, and similar sources.

lion (Capgemini 2019).[12] The rest of the section aims to provide a better understanding of the current philanthropic landscape and its potential for Africa's development. Outside the scope of this chapter are other forms of philanthropy, such as philanthropic activities financed by governments, charitable giving that is not aimed at supporting development, and mobilized philanthropy that brings together many smaller donors or local and in-kind philanthropy which has always been part of communities in Africa.

Philanthropic finance, unlike institutional investors, is not primarily motivated by financial returns but by social impact. Philanthropic actors are not subject to the same pressures as financial investors to deliver minimum financial returns. Instead, they value the social impact of their investments. As such, philanthropy tends to finance socioeconomic causes, such as health, sanitation, universal education, eradication of disease, poverty alleviation, and climate change.

Philanthropic organizations are also more independent and can thus allocate their capital toward riskier ventures. Organizations are not bound by electoral and political cycles. They have great autonomy in decision-making and operations. Their capital is not strictly earmarked for specific uses and, is likely to be more agile in the face of changing conditions and can thus be more easily allocated to more innovative and riskier projects.

Size and Scope of the Investor Base

Philanthropic funds heading to developing countries remain modest and concentrated among a few providers.[13] Limited public data are available on international philanthropic flows. Based on a 2016 survey of 143 foundations, OECD (2018) estimates that private philanthropic flows meant to promote economic development in developing countries averaged $8 billion a year between 2013 and 2015.[14] A recent update based on a smaller sample of 33 foundations finds gross disbursements of the same magnitude in most recent years (OECD 2020d). Another source of data comes from the Foundation Center and the Council on Foundations (2018), which evaluates international giving for US foundations at $9 billion in 2015. All in all, these amounts are small compared to ODA, as measured by the OECD, which averaged about $140 billion a year during 2013–18. They are also miniscule compared to the financial wealth of HNWI, which has increased from

[12]Capgemini defines HNWIs as those who have "investable assets of $1 million or more, excluding primary residence, collectibles, consumables, and consumer durables."

[13]Data on global private giving are much higher. But most of these funds do not leave their home country. Also, private giving can be motivated by objectives other than economic development (for example, religious reasons).

[14]Numbers are based on an OECD survey of 143 foundations.

Figure 51. Global Philanthropic Giving by Recipient Countries' Income Group, 2013–15
(Share of total amount, US dollars)

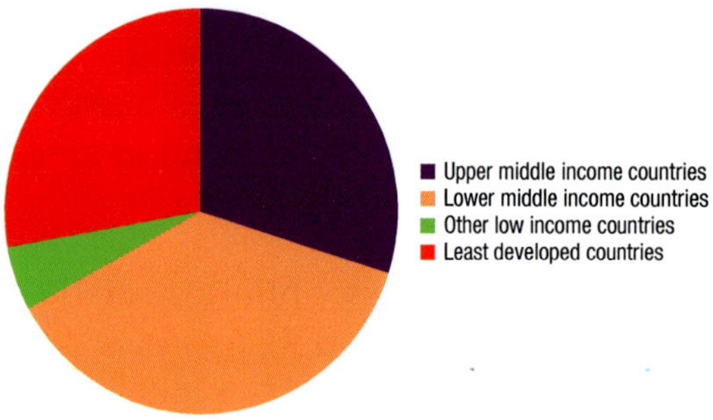

Source: Survey on Private Philanthropy for Development 2013–15: Data questionnaire (OECD 2018).

Figure 52. Global Philanthropic Giving by Sector, 2013–15
(Billions of US dollars)

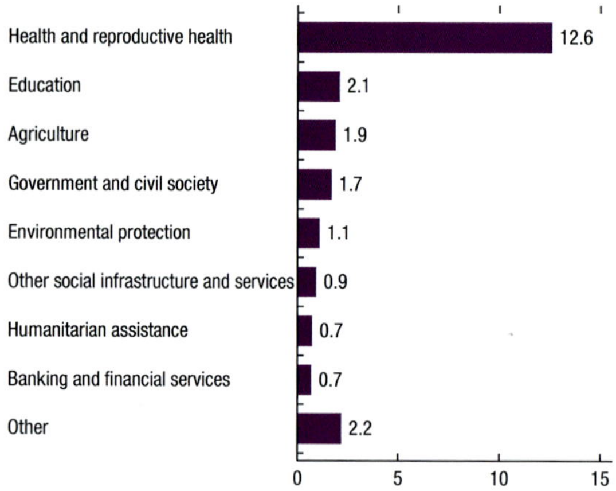

Source: Survey on Private Philanthropy for Development, OECD (2018).

$53 trillion in 2013 to $68 trillion in 2018 (Capgemini 2019). In addition, philanthropy funds are highly concentrated among a few providers. Of the 143 foundations surveyed by OECD (2018), the Bill & Melinda Gates Foundation provided half of total giving during 2013–15. And about 80 percent of the total philanthropic giving was provided by only 20 foundations.

Unlike institutional investors, philanthropies are strongly present in Africa which is the largest recipient of their giving. Philanthropy has a long history in Africa, where traditional local channels are already well established. About 30 percent of global philanthropic finance went to Africa in 2013–15, making it the largest regional recipient (OECD 2018). Preliminary data for 2017–18 estimate this share at one-quarter (OECD 2020d). Giving is concentrated toward middle-income countries, such as Nigeria and South Africa (Figure 51). The preference of foundations for middle-income countries is partly due to the fact that they have a better-established network for engagement, especially nongovernmental organizations (NGOs) and civil society organizations (CSOs), which are the main intermediaries for channeling and implementing the funds (see below).

Philanthropies' engagement has focused mainly on the health sector. More than half of philanthropic giving is concentrated in health, which received $12.6 billion during 2013–15, with the majority of resources dedicated to infectious diseases (Figure 52). Education received the second-largest share, estimated at $2.1 billion. Beyond traditional philanthropy, "venture philanthropy" tends to engage in projects with a more innovative and business-oriented approach by providing not only funding but also technical assistance and capacity building (OECD netFWD 2014, Gianoncelli and others 2019).[15] Venture philanthropists have provided financing for projects that were perceived as risky by other donors. This has been demonstrated in economies in Africa, such as Nigeria and Zimbabwe, wherein local philanthropists teamed up with venture philanthropist to conduct small-scale trial solutions for neglected tropical diseases (Agler 2019).

Many argue that private wealth could make a larger contribution to financing the SDGs. Private philanthropic resources are tackling social issues that other private international flows often cannot reach or have no interest in. Many are beginning to see philanthropy as a key financing source that could help close the SDG funding gap. One avenue to mobilize further philanthropic funding is the Giving Pledge campaign, which aims to convince billionaires to donate at least half their net wealth for charitable causes, including development aid. According to the 2020 billionaire census of Wealth-X, there were 2,825 billionaires worldwide in 2019 owning some $9.4 trillion in assets (Wealth-X 2020). Assuming that the top 15 richest billionaires (with a cumulative wealth close to $1 trillion) commit a quarter of their wealth to achieving the SDGs, this one-off pledge would raise close to $250 billion, yielding an annual flow of $10 billion if invested with a 5 percent return. The size of this annuity remains limited compared to the financing needs described in Chapter 2, which raises the question of the ability of one-off donations to sustain long-term development through durable and stable funding. Many proposals focus on one-off (rather than recurrent) gifts made by the wealthiest. This means that one-off gifts would need to be extremely large to generate sufficient annual returns. An alternative proposal is to invite the wealthiest to contribute annually. For instance, the Move Humanity campaign aims at mobilizing billionaires to donate 1 percent of their net worth each year to finance the SDGs. In this case, the amounts raised would be much higher at almost $100 billion a year.

Attractiveness of Africa for Philanthropic Finance

Africa is a region where philanthropy can have a huge socio-economic impact. Incentives between African governments and philanthropists are very much aligned when it comes to the SDGs. On the one hand, Africa must make considerable progress to meet the SDGs but lacks the resources to do so. The SSA region has at least half of the world's poor, the largest share of fragile countries, and the most acute fiscal and debt sustainability constraints. On the other hand, philanthropists have resources, and they are interested

[15]Venture philanthropy is a type of impact investment that takes concepts and techniques from venture capital finance and business management and applies them to achieving philanthropic goals. A foundation could, for instance, support the activities a charitable startup through tailored seed financing as well as nonfinancial support (for example, coaching the management team on business planning).

in making investments that will have positive socioeconomic and environmental impact.

Informal and community-based giving is deeply embedded in the African culture and could be easily leveraged. Informal philanthropy has a long history in Africa wherein richer households often give away shares of their income through informal transfers to support friends, family, and community members out of a sense of solidarity or social obligation (Schwier and others 2020). In recent decades, however, these transfers have increasingly started to operate through more organized vehicles, such as local institutional foundations engaged in more structured giving, especially in Anglophone Africa (Moyo 2010). The majority of these foundations work in the SDG sectors, such as poverty alleviation, health, and education, among others. These local networks could act as intermediaries to bring international philanthropists closer to local recipients and their needs. The potential is huge for these two forms of philanthropy to complement each other in order to fulfill development priorities.

Bottlenecks to Further Involvement of Philanthropies

The regulatory, legal, and political environment may discourage philanthropic activity in some countries. National legislations in African countries can complicate the activities of international foundations in developing countries by restricting the access of CSOs to international funding (Rutzen 2015, Foundation Center and the Council on Foundations 2018). Regulations governing philanthropy are usually part of legislation either on CSOs or on corporate social investment. Philanthropic giving can thus be subject to unfavorable tax policies (including absence of tax incentives on giving) or restrictions or onerous reporting on receiving foreign funding, especially under anti-money laundering regulations (UNDP 2016). In some cases, perceptions of involvement of foundations with human rights advocacy groups can also create political resistance. Overall, very few African countries have specific strategies to engage with philanthropy, with recent exceptions being Kenya, Rwanda, and South Africa (Moyo 2017, OECD 2018). Mauritius is one of the few African countries with a law on philanthropy.

The lack of coordination and transparent information among stakeholders may lead to overlap in activities and a neglect of eligible recipients. There is little knowledge-sharing and engagement between foundations, ODA providers, governments, and other development organizations (NGOs and CSOs), which limits opportunities for collaboration (OECD 2018a). In many cases, philanthropies are not included in discussions on strategic development priorities including the 2030 SDG agenda. This lack of coordination may lead to unintended overlap between philanthropic organizations and

Figure 53. Average Engagement Period of Global Philanthropic Giving

(Years and percent of total number of foundations)

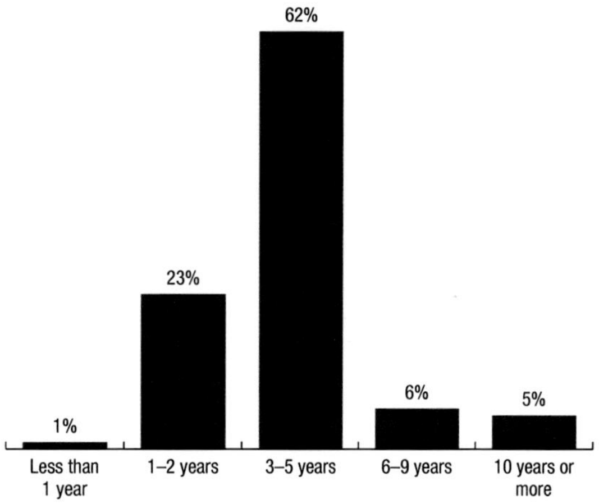

Source: Survey on Private Philanthropy for Development, OECD (2018).

ODA-supported initiatives and as result some groups could be over-serviced, while other could be neglected.

Although the SDGs have turned the spotlight on philanthropic giving, data reporting by foundations is not systematic. In Africa, many actors work in philanthropy. However, there is a lack of comprehensive, robust, and timely reporting regarding their activities (OECD 2018). This lack of detailed data makes it difficult to track the amounts granted, the recipients, and the timing when grants were disbursed. Disclosure of data by foundations is mostly voluntary and may come up against philanthropies' view that they provide funds at their own discretion. Additionally, the lack of data makes evaluation and monitoring of impact of this financing quite limited.

Finally, giving is mostly short-term and focused on stable, middle-income countries, which raises questions about its socioeconomic impact. Philanthropist flows go predominantly to stable, middle-income countries and are implemented through large, established partners, such as international organizations and NGOs. Only a third of the allocated funds go to fragile and low-income countries, which are in greater need of the funds (OECD 2018). Moreover, the large majority of foundations engagement is for five years or less (Figure 53). This short tenure is of a concern, as social investments made by philanthropy in sectors such as eduction or environmental change cannot be sustained through one-off or short-term financing. One-off investment will have only limited impact and is out of step with SDG goals.

Unlocking Resources from Philanthropies

The regulatory environment for philanthropies should facilitate their operation, while not hampering their autonomy. To ensure that philanthropic foundations are able to perform the activities in their mandate, governments may consider granting them with a legal status that would offer them some protection and distinguishes from other CSOs working in non-philanthropic fields (Moyo 2017). This legal status would also make it easier to receive

Figure 54. Channels of Delivery of Global Philanthropic Giving, 2013–15
(Billions of US dollars)

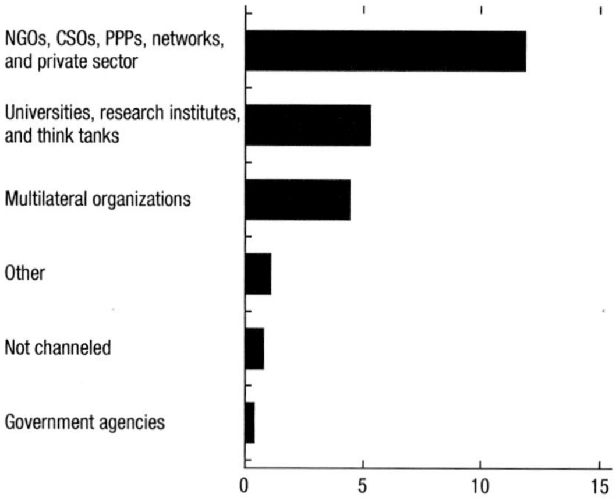

Source: Survey on Private Philanthropy for Development, OECD (2018).

foreign funding while ensuring funds are subject to standard oversight.

Philanthropic organizations could also benefit from a more systematic approach that fosters collaboration with governments and other donors toward achieving the development agenda. On the one hand, national governments would stand to benefit by viewing foundations as development partners as they do with donors. They may also help match philanthropies to relevant causes, in particularly in lower-income economies, which would reduce transactions costs and the misallocation of funds. An example is the Kenya Philanthropy Platform which has created a dialogue to engage with foundations and identify common priorities with the government (OECD netFWD 2017). On the other, better coordination and exchange of information could also help foundations serve more effectively national priorities and ensure complementarity with other initiatives, including local ones.

In particular, better coordination and involvement of the main stakeholders could boost the amount of philanthropic activities in fragile states and low-income countries. The quasi totality of philanthropic giving is implemented through intermediary institutions, with only 3 percent of the funds executed by the foundations themselves. According to the survey conducted by OECD (2018), foundations use predominantly NGOs, CSOs, and private networks (half of total giving); universities, teaching, and research institutions (about 20 percent); and multilateral organizations (about 20 percent) (Figure 54). Only 2 percent of the funds are channeled through government agencies, reflecting a lack of confidence from the foundations regarding the ability of the public sector to implement projects efficiently. This network of intermediaries is less developed in lower income and fragile countries, which is one of the reasons why foundations are less present in these countries that very much need them. In addition to developing these local networks, possible solutions could be to either enhance the role of multilateral organizations as main counterparts of foundations in the poorest countries or for governments to more actively reach out to foundations and convince them that they can be credible partners in the delivery of the services.

Centralized efforts are needed to ensure that data sharing on philanthropic activity is systematic and publicly available. Such efforts would improve strategic planning, better allocation of funding, avoid duplication of efforts and create accountability. Several organizations collect and publish data on philanthropic giving, including OECD netFWD, Candid (formerly Foundation Center) and Worldwide Initiatives for Grantmaker Support. The International Aid Transparency Initiative also provides a platform, which only a few foundations are currently using, to disclose their information, as reporting can be onerous for smaller foundations (OECD 2018).

Fintech innovations can also contribute to catalyzing diaspora philanthropy. In many countries, the crowdfunding model has become a mainstream vehicle for financing private projects and ventures. It is still underdeveloped in SSA, but its potential is large, because of the role of Africa as global leader in mobile money and digital finance, as well as the cultural proximity of crowdfunding with more traditional support systems in the region. The donation model, which represents about one-third of crowdfunding in SSA, could facilitate the delivery of diaspora philanthropy and increase volumes (Box 10).

Finally, lessons should be learned from the successful experience of the Bill & Melinda Gates Foundation in the health sector. The Gates foundation was launched in 2000. Over the last two decades, the foundation has spent $53.8 billion on its various programs, with $39.8 billion going to global development and global health programs. The model of the foundation is not to substitute for direct provision of services by the government, but to provide seed money and impetus for new, innovative, and possibly risky initiatives, such as Gavi, the Vaccine Alliance (Gates 2020). The success of the foundation has come to a large extent from its ability to foster global partnerships and catalyze financing from other sources, including other HNWIs (for example, Warren Buffet), international institutions, and various public and private partners.

The example of the Gates Foundation also suggests that global funds can be a vehicle for international foundations to invest in development sectors. Sachs and Schmidt-Traub (2017) argue that the "global fund" model, successfully used for health (for instance, with the Global Fund to Fight AIDS, Tuberculosis and Malaria), could be replicated in other sectors such as education, sanitation, and rural electrification. Global funds are public-private partnerships that pool funds at the global level and provide performance-based financing for development projects. Their success relies on a few key ingredients: (1) they play a catalytic role to gather international funding at a large scale, and most donors contribute without earmarking, which allows some flexibility in the use of the funds; (2) they foster dialogue and synergies among the main stakeholders through country coordination mechanisms that comprise representatives of the government, civil society, the private sector, donors, and beneficiaries; and (3) they do not implement the programs themselves but select and finance projects based on an independent technical evaluation combined with ex post audit of performance. This model, which creates a simpler channel for foundations and provides guarantees regarding program performance and absence of political interference, could be used more systematically for scaling up philanthropy in Africa.

Other Sources of Private Finance

Beyond institutional investors and philanthropy, other untapped sources and mechanisms for private finance exist. This chapter focuses primarily on institutional investors and philanthropists, who have considerable resources and potential for financing large-scale development projects. However, other solutions and mechanisms exist to either increase the pool of private finance or better channel it to development projects, including smaller ones.

Remittances

Remittances are the largest source of international private finance going to low-income countries. In 2019, remittance flows to low-and middle-income countries exceeded FDIs as the largest source of incoming financial flows, having previously overtaken ODA and private portfolio flows. That year, remittances to these countries reached a record high of $548 billion, slightly larger than FDIs ($534 billion) and ODA ($166 billion), according to World Bank (2020b). Remittances to low and middle-income countries in SSA were estimated at about $50 billion in 2019 (equivalent to almost 3 percent of the region GDP), more than 70 percent higher than the 2009 level.

Remittances are found to have positive effects on development outcomes. By raising household income, remittances can help reduce poverty and smooth private consumption (Adams and Page 2005; Gupta, Pattillo, Wagh 2007). Evidence suggests that recipient households mostly use remittances to finance consumption, such as food and consumer goods, rather than savings or investment, as shown by Chami and others (2005).

However, the potential of remittances is limited by the low degree of financial inclusion. Remittances could potentially enable households to invest in human capital and increase their ownership of durable assets (World Bank 2006a, OECD 2017b). But the impact on savings and investment depends to a large extent on whether remittances can improve the households' credit worthiness and boost their access to financial services. In countries with a low degree of financial inclusion, remittances are less likely to have significant leverage effect on entrepreneurship and longer-term investment decisions. In addition, the beneficiaries of remittances do not necessarily take into account the externalities of their spending; thus, they may tend to underinvest in areas with positive externalities, such as health and education.

Another impediment is the high cost of sending remittances to Africa. It is more expensive to send money to SSA than to any region in the world (though it has become more affordable over time) largely due to a lack of competition. In the third quarter of 2020, senders paid an average of 8.5 percent to transfer money to SSA, a figure that is higher than the average for low- and middle-income countries of 6.8 percent and well above the SDG indicative target of 3 percent (World Bank 2020b).[16]

The COVID pandemic is also likely to durably reduce remittances flows. World Bank (2020b) estimates that remittance flows to low- and middle-income countries declined by about 7 percent in 2020 and could decline by another 7 percent globally in 2021, as the crisis raises unemployment across the world. Remittances to SSA are no exception to this trend: they are estimated to have fallen by about 9 percent 2020 and are expected to decrease by another 6 percent in 2021. The contraction of remittances is partly due to the fact that immigrants are particularly vulnerable to unemployment in migrant-hosting countries, since many have lower-skilled and vulnerable jobs.

Fintech Innovations

The fintech sector has grown very rapidly in SSA in the past decade. Access to financial services has increased massively, with the SSA region becoming the global leader in mobile money services. As discussed in Sy and others (2019), SSA is ahead of other regions in the areas of mobile-money innovation, adoption, and usage.

By boosting financial development and inclusion, fintech has the potential to bring more finance to the private sector. On average, SSA countries have lower levels of financial inclusion and financial sector depth, compared to other parts of the world. A large proportion of the population does not have access to financial services. Only 20 percent of the population has a bank account compared to above 90 percent in advanced economies and about 40 percent in nonadvanced economies.

[16]Remittance costs are typically reported as the average fee, expressed as percentage, of sending $200 abroad.

Fintech innovations provide significant opportunities for private finance. A number of innovations can indeed improve access to financing for private projects:

- *Broad mobile banking services.* While SSA leads other regions in mobile money (payment and money storage services), there is huge demand for other financial services, such as credit provision, cross-border payments, various forms of investment products, and insurance services. More advanced types of fintech, centered on lending rather than payments, are growing throughout SSA.
- *Credit risk assessment.* For SSA banks, the cost of assessing credit risk is relatively high, reflecting unreliable accounting and financial business information, the relative scarcity of credit bureaus and collateral registries, and the size of the informal economy. New technologies, such as big data and machine learning, have the potential to reduce the cost of credit risk assessments and overcome informational barriers, particularly in countries that do not have well-established credit and asset registries.
- *Peer-to-peer lending.* The adoption of crowdfunding tools, where relatively small amounts are raised from a large number of people via internet, is still lagging in SSA compared to other regions. But the potential is high (see Box 10).
- *Cross-border transfers.* Fintech technologies can help bypass the complex and expensive chain of intermediaries intervening in cross-border payments (including remittances). This could provide an alternative to the traditional correspondent banking model and significantly reduce transfer costs to Africa.

Gaps in underlying physical infrastructure and inadequate regulations hinder the growth of fintech in many African countries. Sy and others (2019) provide an overview of the main bottlenecks and risks associated with the development of fintech in the region. The main impediments are the limited and unreliable access to broadband internet connections as well as the poor quality of electricity services in SSA. Addressing infrastructure gaps could lead to higher usage, better assimilation, and a stronger impact of new technologies on private finance and private investment. In addition, fintech innovations may generate risks and vulnerabilities that are not well covered by existing regulations. There are, for instance, concerns regarding financial stability, money laundering, and financing of terrorism. Thus, support for fintech innovations needs to be complemented by a rapid adaptation of regulations and safeguards to identify and manage the new risks.

Sustainable Finance Instruments

The market for sustainable finance offers new opportunities for investors to finance the development-related activities of the corporate sector. A rapidly growing pool of investors has emerged who focus on economic, social, and governance (ESG) considerations in their portfolio decisions. Sustainable finance is not a unique asset class but refers to a multidimensional certification and assessment system that can be applied to any class. Initially, the market developed through negative screening of equity investments, where certain firms or sectors were excluded from investment strategies (for example, tobacco or munitions). It has since grown to include a broad array of fixed-income assets, loans, and alternative investments (for example, private equity and venture capital). They include green bonds, one of the fastest growing segments of the market, where proceeds are used to fund new and existing projects with environmental benefits. Other examples include ESG money market bonds, sustainability bonds, and even traditional corporate bonds that have ESG criteria incorporated into their credit risk (IMF 2019e).

ESG investments in Africa are a very small segment of the overall market. Depending on the definition used, estimates of the size of the global ESG market varies from $3 trillion to $31 trillion (IMF 2019e). Information collected from Africa-based fund managers suggests that the domestic ESG market in Africa is small and largely concentrated in Southern Africa, with total estimated assets under management of about $430 billion in assets in 2017 (GSIA 2019, GSB 2020). Themes for ESG investments in Africa were well aligned with the SDGs, including a focus on agriculture, health, energy, infrastructure, and inclusive finance.[17]

ESG investing can take a broad range of forms. A number of approaches channel funds to the private sector to achieve progress toward meeting the SDGs. A first approach, based on earmarking, uses the levied funds to finance specific SDG-related projects or assets. For instance, use-of-proceed bonds, such as green bonds, social bonds, or sustainability bonds, are issued with this purpose. An alternative financing approach, which does not require earmarking, targets certain firms meeting ESG standards or certain sectors that are considered sustainable. For instance, general-purpose SDG bonds can be issued by firms seeking to finance their broader SDG strategy. Negative targeting is also possible by excluding firms or sectors that do not meet these criteria. A common feature of these two approaches (earmarking versus targeting) is that both require strong corporate governance mechanisms and transparent monitoring of activities and results to ensure the funds are used for the earmarked project or to achieve the broader SDG outcomes (UN 2019). A third approach aims at creating a more direct link between financ-

[17]The estimates of this paragraph include the allocation of funds to both the public and private sectors.

ing and SDG outcomes by linking bond coupon payments to specific and measurables outcomes delivered by the funds' recipient. These types of bonds (called "SDG-linked bonds") can create stronger monitoring and enforcement mechanisms, as coupons would increase if the issuer does not meet clearly defined and observable SDG targets.[18]

The growth of the ESG financing market requires a coordinated approach to developing data standards and monitoring. A central challenge is the limited set of consistent methodologies and reporting norms (IMF 2019e). This is particularly the case in the corporate sector in which data reporting is overwhelmingly voluntary and patchy. Moreover, measuring specific outcomes in the SDG space is challenging due to the longer-term timeline for achieving impact and the interlinkages with other factors such as government policies, reforms, or external shocks. Looking ahead, efforts are needed to (1) achieve consistent corporate reporting using quantified, precise, and well-defined SDG-related indicators; (2) standardize investment terminology and product definitions; and (3) establish clear development standards for the corporate sector and financial products. By developing these cross-market rules and norms, private finance will have the space to develop SDG products in a more transparent market and offer the accountability needed for investors seeking both financial returns and SDG impact.

[18]For example, in 2019 the Italian energy company Enel issued an SDG-linked bond where the coupon payment increased if targets for installed capacity in renewable energy sources were not met.

Box 9. Types of Institutional Investors

By contrast to retail investors, "institutional investors" are large entities pooling money to purchase securities and other assets. This group includes both traditional investors—such as investments funds, insurance companies, and pension funds—and alternative investors, such as hedge funds, private equity firms, exchange-traded funds, and sovereign wealth funds.

The main types of institutional investors are the following:

- *Pension funds* provide individuals with a hedge against the loss of income in their retirement years. A portion of pensioners' savings is invested in bonds, stocks, real estate, and other assets for future investment returns. The portfolio maturity of pensions funds is long (30–40 years) since these funds start collecting contributions when individuals enter the workforce. Their portfolios tend to have more liquid assets than insurance companies but less than banks.
- *Insurance companies* assume risk on behalf of their policyholders in exchange for a premium. These premiums are invested to provide a source of future claims for policy holders and a profit for the insurer. The investment horizon is also relatively long-term (15–20 years).
- *Mutual funds* pool different types of assets (stocks, bonds, cash, and other securities) from multiple investors, which are then invested into a variety of holdings. Investing in such a wide range of stocks and bonds would not be possible for the average investor without the help of a mutual fund.
- *Sovereign wealth funds* are special-purpose investments funds owned by governments. Their main objectives are to preserve public resources (such as oil) for future generations, smooth fiscal revenues, and manage foreign exchange reserves. Funds more focused on fiscal stabilization may show greater preference for fixed income and cash but others tend to prefer returns over liquidity, and typically have a higher risk tolerance compared to other institutional investors.

Sources: BFT BSDC (2018); Della Croce and Yermo (2013); and Çelik and Isaksson (2014).

Box 10. The Potential of Crowdfunding for Philanthropy in Africa

Crowdfunding is still underdeveloped in Africa. Alternative financing sources (crowdfunding as well as other forms of online lending) amounted to $209 million in Africa in 2018, representing less than 0.1 percent of total global volumes (Ziegler and Shneor 2020). This is compared to a 71 percent share for China, 20 percent for the United States, 6 percent for Europe (half of which is in the United Kingdom), 2 percent for Asia-Pacific excluding China, 1 percent for Latin America, and about half a percent for the Middle East. Unlike other regions the majority of crowdfunding coming to Africa is from international sources (close to 80 percent of total), primarily from the United States and the United Kingdom.

Crowdfunding constitutes a vehicle for philanthropic giving, as it enables many contributors to donate or invest small amounts for projects, investments or causes, through an internet platform. While crowdfunding is typically known for investment or reward-based funding of ventures in advanced economies, the "donation-based crowdfunding model" provides a mechanism to advertise and centralize calls for donations, with the objective of gathering funding for social or developmental projects, as well as for humanitarian or crisis response.

Donation-based crowdfunding is the largest crowdfunding model in SSA, accounting for about one-third of all transactions, in contrast to other regions where investment models dominate (Chao and others 2020). International experience shows that the initial development of crowdfunding activities often relies on donation-based models, which precede investment-funding platforms, as perceptions of risk and needs evolve. Positive experiences with donation platforms can provide confidence, reduce risk perception, and ultimately encourage the move towards other forms of crowdfunding, such as peer-to-peer lending and other investment models.

In particular, crowdfunding platforms can provide a low-cost and efficient platform to facilitate diaspora philanthropy (Flanigan 2017). The term "diaspora philanthropy" characterizes situations in which members of the diaspora donate money, goods, or services to their existing network of family and friends back home. Intermediaries often act to help to transfer money back to the home country, which can be through community groups, churches, NGOs, or online platforms to facilitate transfers and build on existing social networks. The benefit of diaspora philanthropy is that it often targets projects or areas in underserved communities wherein traditional donors do not intervene. Community and familial links facilitate also targeting and delivery of philanthropic funds.

Potential to expand crowdfunding in Africa can leverage the large digital and mobile money users in SSA, where financing provided by traditional financial institutions is

Box 10. The Potential of Crowdfunding for Philanthropy in Africa *(continued)*

low. Crowdfunding provides, in particular, an avenue for informal funding for many micro and small enterprises, which may not have access to credit through formal institutions and microfinance (Chao and others 2020)

To fully use the potential of crowdfunding for philanthropy several barriers need to be overcome. While the high utilization of mobile and digital banking in SSA supports the use and expansion of fintech technologies, more-tailored regulation of these platforms is needed to provide certainty for lenders and recipients. The African Crowdfunding Association was established in 2015 to facilitate legislation and public awareness of crowdfunding. In addition, although the high use of mobile and digital services is promising in SSA, the internet infrastructure remains an impediment to realizing the benefits and uptake of crowdfunding models for both philanthropic and investment purposes.

CHAPTER

7 Conclusion: A New Development Paradigm for African Countries?

The COVID-19 pandemic threatens to reverse Africa's hard-won socioeconomic gains of the last two decades. The pandemic has brought economic activity to a standstill in 2020 and is set to cause a spike in poverty and inequality. The crisis has also accentuated fiscal pressures, further reducing the fiscal space and raising debt risks, at a time when spending on health and other infrastructure is more important than ever.

In this difficult environment, development strategies need a rethink. In recent years, many SSA countries have been relying on public-investment-driven growth, and public debt has increased significantly. This trend is not sustainable, absent significant changes in domestic revenue mobilization and official assistance. And, in any event, most SSA countries would benefit from shifting toward more private-sector-driven growth and investment models given demographics and the need for massive job creation.

To ensure that sustainable development goals are matched with sustainable financing sources, private investment has a critical role to play in Africa. The contribution of investors to financing private infrastructure in the region is still very limited, given the needs and compared to other regions. Almost all the infrastructure projects are conducted and financed by the public sector. Risk-adjusted returns of projects in Africa are often perceived by international investors as less attractive than elsewhere in the world. Therefore, mobilizing additional private finance for development will require innovative solutions to improve the risk-return profile of projects.

A fundamental question for policymakers and donors willing to advance development goals is whether to use public funds for traditional public investment or as seed money to incentivize private investment. A portion of taxes or donors' funds could, indeed, be reallocated to promote private projects by providing subsidies or guarantees to investors, as is done in PPPs or blending arrangements. The aim of these incentive measures is to generate a leverage effect, unlocking private investment that would not have otherwise occurred. They could also generate efficiency gains and improve service quality, especially in countries where public delivery has failed to meet minimum standards. On the other hand, ill-designed public incentives can be ineffective (when poorly targeted), costly, possibly distortionary, and generate contingent liabilities. Therefore, caution is advised when reallocating scarce public resources to riskier but possibly transformational uses.

The choice between these two approaches and more generally the balance between public and private finance, needs to pay heed to the country context. In the broadest of terms, two groups of African countries—frontier markets and low-income countries/fragile states—could be distinguished:

- *Frontier markets*—countries with relatively strong state capacity and institutions, already at or close to middle-income level, and with market access—such as Ghana, Kenya, or Senegal—are more attractive to international investors and could benefit more significantly from programs meant to catalyze and incentivize private finance. Their pipeline of bankable projects is already well developed, and many projects have a critical size that make them appealing to investors. Frontier markets are also more advanced in the transition from public to private infrastructure, which is a feature of economic development.[1]
- *Low-income countries and fragile states* have a smaller economic size and tend to have weaker capacity and institutions, including those meant to promote private sector activities. These countries are also less likely to attract international investors, given the smaller scale of projects, asymmetries of information, and high-perceived exit risks. In this case, the scope for private finance mobilization is likely to be more limited, especially in social and physical infrastructure. Attracting more official aid and channeling it to government budgets, while improving public expenditure efficiency, may be a safer and more actionable way of fostering growth and investing in necessary infrastructure.[2]

[1]For instance, ADB (2000), drawing lessons from the experience of PPPs in the road sector in Asia in the 1990s, argued that private sector participation in this sector would benefit most countries that have (1) political leadership and commitment to the private sector participation strategy, (2) political stability, (3) an income level that is not too low, (4) a sound macroeconomy with low and stable inflation and a stable exchange rate, (5) some development of domestic capital markets, and (6) a program of projects.

[2]This does not mean that the poorest and most fragile countries would not benefit from greater private sector participation. But, in difficult environments, mobilizing private finance would require a stronger involvement of DFIs (to build a pipeline of viable projects and catalyze donors' subsidies for private investment within blending arrangements) as well as a radical change in the international narrative on fragile states (emphasizing their demographic potential, for instance).

Any transition from public to private finance in development sectors needs to be gradual and supported by sound institutions. A number of institutional weaknesses and capacity constraints commonly found in developing countries may greatly reduce the benefits from greater private sector participation. A strong regulatory environment and a robust institutional framework are key to mobilizing private entities in the financing and provision of infrastructure, including through PPPs, in a sustainable and efficient way (Romero 2015).

Annex 1. The Choice between Public and Private Finance

The choice between public and private finance depends to a large extent on the size and type of returns generated by a project. To analyze this choice, this annex relies on a stylized framework centered around the provider of development-related services; for instance, a school, hospital, or highway. The provider can be a government unit or a market producer outside the government. The provision of the services generates both private and social returns.[1] The relative size of these two types of returns is a key factor (but not the only one) to determine whether a project is likely to be private or public.

Projects that generate high private returns are generally financed and implemented by the private sector, whereas the government is usually better positioned to carry out projects with high social returns but low private returns. Three main cases can be distinguished, depending on the relative size of private versus social returns:

- *Purely private projects.* If a project generates high cash flows and high private returns, private providers have incentives to produce the services, even without receiving any public subsidy. Service providers should not face large constraints to raise financing from the private sector, since the elevated private returns generate enough revenue to pay high interest and dividends on their liabilities. Thus, the private sector is likely to produce and finance the services. Risk and responsibilities are within the private sector. When the project requires debt, it is recorded as private debt.

[1]"Private returns" denote the returns appropriated by the service provider; they are generated from the sale of the services and possibly from financial support received from the government (which could take multiple forms, including subsidies or tax breaks). "Social returns" denote the broader social benefits shared by the society—benefits that do not accrue solely to the service producer. A gap can exist between social and private returns due to several factors, including externalities, market structure characteristics, and poor governance.

- *Purely public projects.* Some projects have very low (or no) private return and large social returns—a situation described in the literature as a "spill-over gap" (Jaffe 1998). Provided that the government has some fiscal space and costs are not too high, the government has strong incentives to produce these services, financed from the budget, by resorting to taxation or by borrowing from the private sector. In some cases, the spillover gap may be so large that public provision becomes the only realistic option.[2] These projects are public, since risks and responsibilities are within the public sector. Their financing raises government debt.
- *Intermediate cases.* Some projects lie in between these two extreme cases. The projects are initially not attractive to the private sector (both in terms of provision and financing) but could become attractive if the government provides sufficient financial incentives to bring private returns above the investors' hurdle rate. Public support, meant to catalyze private participation and financing, can take the form of a direct transfer, a tax break, financing at below-market rates, or a guarantee. Whether these projects are recorded as public or private depends in the end on who carries most risks and has control (see guidance on sectorization in the IMF *Government Finance Statistics Manual 2014*). It is a qualitative assessment since these arrangements allocate responsibilities and risks between the public and the private sector. In these intermediate cases, financing may impact both public and private debts.

[2]Note that the government may be willing to provide the service for reasons other than high social returns, since other types of market failures can justify public intervention. For instance, if there is a natural monopoly, the private return may be excessively high, and this could justify the public sector taking over (IMF 2004).

Annex 2. An Analysis of Past Private Investment Surges

To assess the scope for more private finance in SSA, this annex analyzes the evolution of private investment over the past decade in a global sample of 170 countries. Annex Figure 2.1 shows the distribution of the change in the private investment ratio between 2007 and 2017, which is the latest year available in the IMF investment database.[1] Over the period, the private investment ratio was, on average, broadly stable in the global sample.

This annex identifies countries that were able to raise their private investment ratio by at least 6 percent of GDP between 2007 and 2017. The analysis focuses on a single decade, since this is the time horizon of the SDGs (to be achieved by 2030). The 6 percent of GDP threshold is used for two main reasons. The first one is purely qualitative: if the three main stakeholders (governments, international community, and private investors) have to contribute in equal manners to closing the SDG gaps—estimated in Chapter 2 at 19 percent of GDP for the median SSA country—this would imply that the private sector should bear one-third of these costs, which is approximately 6 percent of GDP. The second reason refines further the analysis using the estimates provided in Chapter 2: when the potential from all public sources is summed up (5 percent of GDP for domestic revenue mobilization, 2–3 percent of GDP for government expenditure efficiency reforms, and 4–5 percent of GDP from scaling up official aid), the financing gap, relative to the 19 percent of GDP expenditure needs, would also represent about 6 percent of GDP. Thus, a natural question is whether the private sector could cover all or part of this gap over a decade.

Few countries have succeeded in raising private investment significantly over the past decade. Focusing on "successful" cases, only 15 countries out of 162

[1]The IMF "Investment and Capital Stock Dataset, 2020 Update" is available at https://infrastructuregovern.imf.org/content/PIMA/Home/PimaTool.html

Annex Figure 2.1. Distribution of the Change in the Private Investment Ratio between 2007 and 2017
(Global sample)

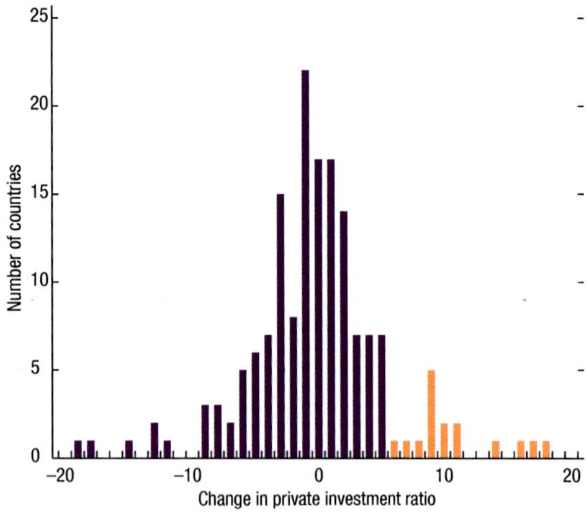

Source: IMF staff calculations based on IMF Investment and Capital Stock Dataset, 2019.
Note: Orange color represents number of countries with private investment ratio increases above 6 percentage points.

Annex Figure 2.2. Countries with a Private Investment Ratio Surge between 2007 and 2017
(Percentage points of GDP)

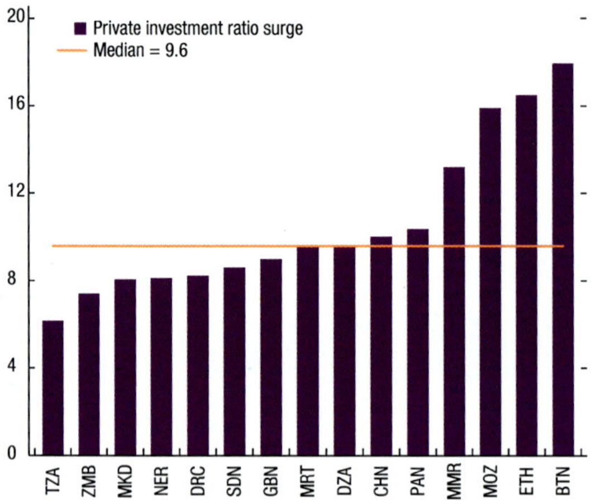

Source: IMF staff calculations based on IMF Investment and Capital Stock Dataset, 2019.
Note: Countries where private investment ratio increased by at least 6 percentage points of GDP over the period. Data labels in the figure is International Organization for Standardization (ISO) country codes.

raised their private investment ratio by at least 6 percentage points during 2007–17 (Annex Figure 2.2, Annex Table 2.1). The median (resp. simple average) increase in these 15 countries was 9.6 (resp. 10.6) percentage points. And this group of countries accounted for about one-fifth of those that were able to register any positive increase in their private investment ratio. Among the best performers, half were from SSA and two-thirds were LIDCs.[2] As shown in Annex Table 2.1, restricting the analysis to developing countries does not change much the results.

Excluding commodity exporters, even fewer countries achieved a large increase in private investment over the decade. The previous exercise is repeated by excluding commodity exporters, since this group may have experienced investment surges in commodity-related sectors that have ambiguous or even negative impact on economic development. Also, these countries typically experience investment cycles that are linked to the fluctuations of commodity prices, making it more difficult to pursue development goals. Only 10 non-commodity exporters were able to increase private investment by at least 6 percentage points during the period 2007–17. In this subgroup, the median increase was comparable to that of the whole sample (including commodity exporters), at about 10.1 percentage points, with the group being

[2]This annex uses the term "best performer" to describe any country that was able to increase its private investment-to-GDP ratio by at least 6 percentage points over the period considered.

Annex Table 2.1. Increase in Private Investment Ratios Over One Decade (2007–17) and Two Decades (1997–2017)

	Full Country Sample			
	One decade		Two decades	
	Global sample	Developing countries only	Global sample	Developing countries only
No. of countries	162	125	162	125
Simple average increase	−0.7	−0.1	1.6	2.2
Median increase	−0.9	−0.3	2.0	2.4
	Subsample of Best Performers			
	One decade		Two decades	
	Global sample	Developing countries only	Global sample	Developing countries only
No. of countries	15	15	33	33
Simple average increase	10.6	10.6	11.2	11.2
Median increase	9.6	9.6	10.0	10.0

Note: Best performers are the countries that succeeded in raising their private investment ratio by at least 6 percentage points of GDP. One decade refers to the period 2007–17 while two decades refers to the period 1997–17.
Source: IMF staff calculations based on IMF Investment and Capital Stock Dataset, 2017.

split between LICs (seven countries, five of which are from SSA) and EMEs (three countries).

Scaling up private investment ratio by at least 6 percentage points seems more feasible over a period of two decades. The analysis is now extended to the past two decades, by looking at the evolution between 1997 and 2017 (Annex Table 2.1). Over these two decades, the number of countries that were able to ramp up private investment by at least 6 percentage points of GDP more than doubles to 33, of which 25 were noncommodity exporters. This corresponds to about a quarter of developing countries. In this sample of best performers, the median increase is not much larger than for the single decade analysis. The reason for the similarity of results between the two analyses is twofold: first, the best performers over the past decade recorded on average relatively minor private investment increases in the penultimate decade; second, most of the additional countries identified with the two-decade analysis (relative to the one-decade analysis) had experienced private investment increases only mildly larger than the threshold of 6 percentage points.

Results are robust to changes in the start and end dates of the sample. The previous exercise, carried out between 1997 and 2017, could be sensitive to the choice of the time period. In particular, results could be affected by the fact that the year 1997 marked the end of the credit boom in Asia. Thus, the exercise is repeated using 10-year averages for the start and end dates instead of single years. For the one-decade analysis, the authors compute the change between the average investment ratio during 1998–2007 and the

Annex Table 2.2. Increase in Private Investment Ratios Over One and Two Decades (Using Averages)

	Full Country Sample			
	One decade		Two decades	
	Global sample	Developing countries only	Global sample	Developing countries only
No. of countries	177	140	176	139
Simple average increase	1.2	1.9	1.2	3.2
Median increase	1.1	1.7	2.0	3.0
	Subsample of Best Performers			
	One decade		**Two decades**	
	Global sample	Developing countries only	Global sample	Developing countries only
No. of countries	18	18	41	39
Simple average increase	8.7	8.7	10.4	10.5
Median increase	8.1	8.1	9.0	9.2

Note: Best performers are countries that succeeded in raising their private investment ratio by at least 6 percentage points of GDP. One decade refers to the period between 1998/07–2008/17 while two decades refers to the period 1988/97–2008/17.
Source: IMF staff calculations based on IMF Investment and Capital Stock Dataset, 2017.

average ratio during 2008–17. For the two-decade analysis, the comparison is between the average 1988–97 and the average 2008–17. Annex Table 2.2 shows that the results are not significantly affected, with still about 10 percent of the countries being "successful" over a one-decade period and a bit more than a quarter over two decades.[3]

A realistic but still-ambitious target for SSA countries could be to raise their private investment ratio by 3 percentage points over the next decade, which would be more in line with what good performers have achieved in the past. Replicating the analysis underlying Annex Table 2.1 with this lower threshold, we find that a quarter of developing countries (29 out of 125) have lifted their private investment ratio by at least 3 percentage points over the past decade, compared to about 10 percent (15 countries) with a 6-percentage-point threshold.

[3]Another robustness analysis based on shorter averages confirms these two orders of magnitude.

Annex 3. Orbis Calculations and Data Cleaning

Chapter 3 uses data from the Orbis Bureau van Dijk database, which is a firm-level database of more than 280 million public and private firms globally, covering 1984–2018. The data set includes both listed and unlisted firms. Several filtering and cleaning techniques were applied for the analysis, which covers 2000–17, 90 countries, and more than 1 million observations overall, with 200,000 foreign owned.

To restrict the size of the data set the authors include only firms from emerging market and developing economies (EMDEs), and exclude all firms in Advanced Economies being less comparable to firms in SSA with different business and investment environment. The authors drop government-owned firms; all other ownership types are retained to ensure focus on private ownership and investment. To identify firms with foreign investment, the authors define a dummy to identify when the global ultimate owner (GUO) is different from the domestic ultimate owner (DUO).[1] The analysis presented in Chapter 3 is based on foreign-owned firms only.

The data set was cleaned to remove errors and outliers in the data, including firms without total assets information, missing or negative employees, and missing NACE industry codes. Firms with observations of return on equity in the top and bottom 1 percent were also removed. Firms were kept in the sample even if year observations were not consecutive, resulting in an unbalanced panel. Annex Table 3.1 details the observations by industry and region.

[1]Bureau Van Dijk ownership definitions. https://www.bvdinfo.com/en-us

Annex Table 3.1. Orbis Data, Number of Firms in Database Used for Analysis, 2000–2017

	Developing Asia	Developing Europe	Latin America and Caribbean	Middle East and North Africa	Sub-Saharan Africa	Total
Countries	16	10	18	20	26	90
All firms	289,372	707,222	7,135	12,004	6,665	1,022,398
All with Foreign Ownership	114,267	83,779	3,534	1,445	1,435	204,460
Agriculture	485	3,130	87	17	82	3,801
Manufacturing	88,362	20,155	1,341	525	706	111,089
Mining	1,885	1,343	127	151	63	3,569
Services	21,070	52,483	1,705	630	543	76,431
SDG-Education	41	370	3	18	15	447
SDG-Electricity	726	815	98	21	12	1,672
SDG-Health	84	518	0	17	0	619
SDG-Infrastructure	1,001	4,563	171	65	3	5,803
SDG-Water	613	402	2	1	11	1,029

Source: Orbis database; and IMF staff.

Annex 4. Sectoral Policies

Transportation[1]

Since the 1990s, transportation has undergone major transformations in Africa. The sector has been partly deregulated, and transport policies have been modified to permit market-determined decisions, enterprise autonomy, and private participation in the ownership and management of transportation businesses. Most bus and trucking companies have been privatized, and governments have made concessions on railways, ports and harbors, and airports, especially since the 2000s. Various forms of public-private partnerships have been tried for airports, seaports, and railways, and to a lesser extent, roads.

Some policies can support private sector involvement in transportation:

- Legal and regulatory restrictions to private sector participation in transport infrastructure need to continue to be lifted.
- PPPs are a tool for delivering transport infrastructure that is in the "public interest" through a thorough strategic analysis and project evaluation conducted by the government. If investment decisions are solely devolved to market forces, the delivery of some infrastructure may not be coherent with broader transport programs. Thus, project finance can come only after effective, sector-wide strategic planning has identified the most defensible projects.

See "The Knowledge Lab" for a comprehensive overview of private sector involvement in various sectors of the economy. The PPP Knowledge Lab was launched in 2015 by the Asian Development Bank, European Bank for Reconstruction and Development, Inter-American Development Bank, Islamic Development Bank, and World Bank Group, with the support from Public–Private Infrastructure Advisory Facility.

[1]Sources: ADB (2000); Butler and Lee (2013); Jerome (2008); Menzies and Mandri-Perrott (2010); Rall, Reed, and Farber (2010); Zegras (2003).

- The decision to pursue an infrastructure PPP should be supported by a comprehensive project analysis (including value for money analysis, public sector comparator, careful assessment of the risks etc.) showing that, over the duration of the contract, a PPP is truly a better option for the state than traditional project delivery and that the project is viable over the long term.
- Screening potential bidders is important in the context of transportation PPPs. Given the generally large size of the projects, private operators should be willing to risk a substantial amount of capital early in the project and have financial strength to overcome expected or unexpected problems.
- The government should identify good projects and then subject those to competitive and transparent bidding. Securing competition for the market is achieved through clear and fair bidding and project selection processes with simple and explicit evaluation criteria.
- Because roads require significant land, the government will need to be involved to secure land for the road. This can often be politically costly and technically difficult to achieve due to poor land registration. In addition to the time required for procurement, this long lead time can reduce the willingness of the private sector to take on the risk. Sufficient preparation by the government can help alleviate concerns.
- Transport infrastructure projects are fraught with risks throughout their life cycle. These risks include permitting and land acquisition risks, risks of cost and time overruns during construction, operation and management, demand and revenue risks, inflation and currency risks, among others. How these risks are allocated between the private sector and the government has important implications for project selection and project performance. Some level of risk should be assumed by the government, although an unbalanced allocation of risks should be avoided (for example, with a general revenue guarantee that would defeat the purpose of using infrastructure PPPs and create large fiscal risks for the government).
- A primary risk is that, once infrastructure is built, private operators will not be able to collect tolls for usage. Political resolve is required to support the introduction of tolling and periodic increases if needed.
- As in other sectors, the government needs to establish a robust legal framework (property rights, contract obligations, security rights, etc.) and regulatory regime (autonomous, independent). Regulation is needed to ensure that quality of service does not deteriorate (especially when little competition for the infrastructure service exists), and to make sure that the infrastructure remains well maintained throughout the life of the contract (especially toward the end of the concession term). An independent reg-

ulatory body, free from the strong lobbying power of industry and with well-defined access to the necessary information, is essential.

Water and Sanitation[2]

Private investment in the water sector remains limited due to equity considerations (which constrain the ability to apply cost-recovery tariffs for water services since access has to be provided to all households independent of their ability to pay) and high fixed costs coupled with long-term irreversible investments that characterize the sector. Private investors are often reluctant to enter the sector without some level of certainty regarding the utilities' capacity to implement tariff revisions, collect revenues, and obtain regular funding from public authorities. Nonetheless, some countries have delegated water services to private operators via PPPs and management contracts for efficiency reasons as private operators are incentivized to improve performance to generate profits. In addition, contrary to common perceptions, two-thirds of the financing for water and sanitation in developing countries originates from household sources via tariffs and self-supply (for example, households' investments in toilets and wells).

Some policies can support private sector involvement in water and sanitation:

- Sector regulation can contribute to reinforce accountability and clarify the roles and responsibilities of the different stakeholders. For instance, distinguishing sector oversight from service provision is usually required to better align incentives and provide the necessary autonomy for service providers. Water regulation, which addresses elements such as tariffs, service quality standards, competition, consumer protection, and pro-poor regulation, need to be transparent and applied independently of political interferences.
- Introducing and monitoring key performance indicators can be a way to trigger efficiency gains and make utilities more attractive to private investors. There is significant room to improve the technical and financial performance of water utilities in Africa through operational efficiency reforms (reduction of leaks, better enforcement of rates collection, more timely maintenance, use of technology, etc.). Partnerships should be rooted in strong accountability mechanisms through clear and consistent output-based contractual arrangements, monitoring and relations based on information-sharing and on consultation with stakeholders.
- To achieve equity objectives and universal access, public subsidies are usually required, such as reduced tariffs and block tariffs structures (that is, highly subsidizing the first few cubic meters to cover basic needs).

[2]Sources: OECD (2009); UN (2018); and World Bank (2006b).

Power[3]

Historically, public utilities in developing countries have generated and distributed electricity and funded their operations and capital investments from end-users, subsidies by the public sector, and development assistance. In recent decades, many African countries have increased private sector participation in the sector, primarily in electricity generation since transmission and distribution networks have natural monopoly characteristics. With recent changes in technology and regulation, decentralized energy solutions, such as mini-grids and off-grids, have enabled new forms of private investments, either from enterprises or households directly. While the objectives of private sector participation in transmission and generation often focus on mobilizing capital for new investments, the main motivation for distribution is generally to improve operational and financial performance of networks already in place.

Some policies can support private sector involvement in the power sector:

- New or updated laws may be needed to enable private participation in the energy sector, as it is legally restricted in some cases. Even if independent power producers can enter legally, other barriers such as lack of access to transmission facilities limit their scale and impact.
- Private sector participation strategies are preferably implemented in stages. Countries typically begin with private investment in power generation, building the legal, financial, and technical capabilities that are prerequisite to more advanced stages of private participation in transmission, distribution, and retail.
- Adopting plans to unbundle the power sector—both vertically (by separating generation, transmission, distribution, and retail functions) and horizontally (by separating functions into multiple competing entities, where possible)—enables potentially competitive segments (generation and retail) to attract private participation.
- The financial sustainability of private sector involvement typically requires tariff increases and a credible commitment to future adjustments, since below-cost pricing is widespread in developing countries.
- Private investors in power generation can be discouraged by the chronic financial difficulties of potential off-takers (for example, state-owned power distribution firms). Power distribution (and to a smaller extent transmission) is often described as the weakest link in the energy sector due to difficulties in bill collection, theft, and other technical constraints hampering

[3]Sources: ESMAP (2015); Hertzmark (2008); Power Futures South Africa (2019); UN (2018).

cash flow generation. This calls for stronger governance and more transparency to strengthen the operations of state-owned enterprises.

- Private sector participation is often associated with a rationalization of processes in utilities and, in particular, staff reduction. Although this improves productivity and layoffs are small relative to national unemployment, measures to mitigate the effects should be put into place.
- Success depends on the willingness of private investors to use the efficiency gains generated to build new capacity, which is not automatic. Experience with PPPs in power distribution suggests that private sector participation is not systematically associated with an increase in investment. One possible option to address this could be to include well designed investment targets into the PPP contracts.
- Governments need to support the energy transition. Mechanisms to encourage renewable energy investments include tax incentives and feed-in tariffs (although, as the price difference between technologies decreases and, in some cases, is eliminated, the need for such mechanisms will decline).

Healthcare[4]

Private healthcare providers (both for-profit and not-for-profit; and formal and informal) play a significant role in developing countries. According to World Bank (2011), more than half of healthcare spending in SSA comes from private parties. In the poorest countries, the private sector is a central provider through traditional practitioners and pharmacists. Engaging existing private providers and increasing private activities can help expand access and coverage, raise the service quality, enhance efficiency, and improve health outcomes. In addition, by providing overall stewardship of health markets, governments can work toward ensuring that the private sector operates in a way that is consistent with the country's health objectives and public interest.

Some policies can support private sector involvement in healthcare:

- Well-performing mixed delivery systems have ongoing, transparent communication (dialogue and information exchange) between government officials involved in health policy and private healthcare providers. This communication leads to better monitoring and better policy design by taking account of private healthcare providers' perspectives and likely reactions to policy initiatives. For the private health sector, forming credible associations or representative organizations is an essential first step to engage in this dialogue.

[4]Sources: Lagomarsino, Nachuk, and Singh Kundra (2009); World Bank (2003b, 2011).

- Effective health systems with substantial private delivery also rely on a specific framework for regulation of the private health sector, which ensures quality and efficiency of care, while protecting public interest. In developing countries, it is often necessary to simplify existing rules and bring them into alignment with what can be enforced. For instance, there are often burdensome and unnecessary costs to register an organization as well as problems obtaining access to critical inputs.
- A clear financing framework needs to be in place for determining the revenues available to the private health sector, such as a health insurance allowing reimbursement for treatment received in a private facility or a system of service contracts between the government and private providers. The financing framework should create incentives for providers to deliver quality services, while minimizing out-of-pocket payments by pooling risks across populations. Public funds need to buy value for money from the best providers—either public or private—that compete on a level playing field (principle of strategic purchasing).
- Like in education, an assessment of affordability is critical for all public-private projects in healthcare, since the government is likely to be responsible, at least partially, for payment of services or other types of support to the private sector.
- A mechanism should allow low-income citizens to have access to quality services from the private sector, such as targeted payment for these services by the government and specific regulations.
- Governments should educate and incentivize patients to demand the most beneficial services. This can increase the supply of high-quality services by private providers and reduce inappropriate provider behavior.
- Technological innovations such as medical advice call centers, telemedicine, mobile diagnostic devices, and healthcare kiosks, create new opportunities for the private sector, while increasing efficiency and providing higher quality and more consistent care to hard-to-reach populations.

Education[5]

The role of the private sector in providing education includes a mix of for profit, nonprofit, and faith-based organizations. In sub-Saharan Africa, provision of education by the private sector has increased markedly over the last 15 years, accounting in 2018 for about 15 percent of primary school enrollment, 20 percent of secondary school enrollment, and 30 percent for tertiary

[5]Sources: Lewis (2013); Lusk-Stover and Patrinos (2015); World Bank (2010, 2014).

education.[6] The main rationale for involving the private sector is to expand access to schooling and improve learning outcomes. Private involvement in education can help increase the level of financial resources committed to the sector and supplement the limited capacity of government institutions to absorb growing demand. While the government must provide stewardship for the whole education system, this does not imply that the state always needs to be the direct provider and financer of all educational services. The private sector can also help to diversify the provision of tertiary education if it is appropriately regulated and to provide quality.

Some policies can support private sector involvement in education:

- Countries need to establish strong regulatory policies to ensure high-quality delivery, accountability, and equity, with a view to providing the government with ultimate control over educational outcomes.
- Governments should enable a variety of providers to enter the market, as this will increase client power and enable citizens to make informed choices about where to send their children.
- An assessment of affordability is essential in public-private education projects since the government is often responsible for funding part of the private schools' expenses.
- Measures could be taken to enhance accountability of private providers, such as making information on the quality of services available to all families and implementing a system of rewards/sanctions based on schools' admissions policies and learning outcomes.
- Protection for vulnerable groups can be achieved through targeted funding strategies (for example, tax subsidies, scholarships, and cash transfers), limiting student fees in private schools that receive some public funding, and regulating school admission practices.
- In the tertiary sector, the regulatory framework governing the sector should set out the requirements for the establishment of institutions and programs, the accreditation of degrees and teachers, and the criteria for evaluation to ensure quality provision.

[6]Data on private school enrollment are available from the Word Bank World Development Indicators database. Data for tertiary education are less comprehensive.

Annex 5. Structure of the General Equilibrium Model

Description of the Model

The model used in the simulations presented in Chapter 5 is a dynamic general equilibrium that includes a continuum of households facing idiosyncratic risk (as is common in the inequality literature) and also multiple sectors with frictions preventing the movement of factors across sectors (as is typical in the structural transformation literature).

The model describes a small open economy with five consumption goods: domestic food, imported food, manufacturing, services, and energy.

There are several predetermined and fixed types of households: (1) rural and urban, (2) private sector and government employees, (3) entrepreneurs (capital holders), and (4) low-skilled and high-skilled workers. There is a continuum of households, equal ex ante, but facing uninsurable idiosyncratic risk. Households solve dynamic optimization problems taking prices and government policies as given.

The model includes five sectors, each characterized by different technologies: agriculture products–domestic and exported (with rural households, employing land and low-skilled labor); manufacturing (with a technology using low-skilled labor, energy and capital, owned by entrepreneurs); services (produced either by urban households in family businesses, with low-skilled labor; or by entrepreneurs in the industrial sector, with high-skilled labor and energy); and energy (with a capital intensive technology). Annex Table 5.1 summarizes the relationships between goods, producers, what is an input, and the use of the different goods in this economy.

The only financial assets available are one-period bonds, and they are traded among households to allow for risk sharing. The interest rate on these bonds,

Annex Table 5.1. Structure of the Economy

Goods	Producer	Input	Use
Agricultural goods	Agricultural workers	Land, labor, fertilizer	Consumption, and input production of agricultural exports
Manufacturing	Entrepreneurs	Private sector labor, capital, and energy	Consumption, investment, exports
Services	Private/public sector workers Entrepreneurs	Informal technology Private sector labor, capital and energy	Consumption, investment
Electricity	SOE/Private Sector Entrepreneurs	Capital	Consumption, Tradable
Agricultural export	Entrepreneurs	Domestic food product, private sector labor	Export

Source: IMF staff.

the wage for public and private employees, the price of domestic food, and the price of services are determined by domestic supply and demand forces in equilibrium.

The price of energy is exogenously given (can be thought as a policy variable), and a wedge is introduced between the price perceived for energy use and the income per unit obtained by producers. This wedge implements rationing in the model as the higher total cost per unit of energy for users reduces the quantity demanded. The size of the wedge is determined in equilibrium, such that, given the price, the quantity demanded equals the quantity produced.

Different scenarios are analyzed by comparing the baseline versus the steady state of the model under the parameters of the scenario under consideration (holding all other parameters fixed). Hence, the numbers reported should be interpreted as medium-term effects (in simulations not reported here, the model reaches values close to steady state in about seven years).

Functional Specification for Preferences and Production

Each type of household maximizes expected utility

$$U = E\sum_{t=0}^{+\infty} \beta^t u(c_t)$$

in which

$$u(c_t^f, c_t^e, c_t^o) = \frac{(c_t^f - \ddot{a})^{1-\sigma}}{1-\sigma} + \gamma\frac{(c_t^e)^{1-\sigma}}{1-\sigma} + \omega\frac{(c_t^o)^{1-\sigma}}{1-\sigma}$$

And (f) stands for food, energy, and other goods. In turn, food is a combination of domestically produced food (a) and imports (*), while (o) is a similar composite of traded and non-traded goods.

$$c_t^f = [\epsilon(c_t^a)^\rho + (1 - \epsilon)(c_t^*)^\rho]^{\frac{1}{\rho}}$$

Production technologies are assumed to be Cobb-Douglas in the different inputs used. For example, the entrepreneur technology for non-tradeable goods (super index n), which requires electricity (e), capital (k), and labor (h) with total factor productivity (z) is given by:

$$y^{n,ent} = z^{n,ent}\left((k_t^n)^\alpha (e_t^n)^{1-\alpha}\right)^{\alpha^n} (h_t^n)^{1-\alpha^n}$$

Calibration of the Model

The analysis is based on an illustrative economy, considered to be similar in features to a representative African economy (non-agricultural commodity exporters). Alternative illustrative groups were considered, finding similar results (agricultural commodity exporters or economies with a larger urban presence). Non-agricultural commodity exporters have 50 percent of their labor force in rural areas, and non-agricultural commodities constitute 15 percent of GDP.

Some of the key parameters of the model are exogenously defined (using data of the illustrative group, and other standard values in the literature—for example, discount rates, risk aversion, and capital shares) and are listed in Annex Table 5.2.

Other parameters are set so that the steady state of the model satisfies the following. Consumption to GDP represents 68 percent. In turn, services account for 62 percent of consumption, energy 4 percent, and the rest going to traded goods. Investment accounts for 8 percent of GDP. The Gini is 52 in equilibrium, with higher urban inequality (a Gini of 54). In terms of shares of gross output, agriculture accounts for 41 percent, manufacturing for 12 percent, services 40 percent, and the reminder 7 percent is attributed to electricity production. Finally, total government revenues are about 25 percent of GDP, of which 11 percentage points are obtained from value-added tax. Effective income tax rates are 12 percent on average.

Annex Table 5.2. Calibration of Parameters

Variables	Parameters	Value
Preferences		
Discount Rate	β	0.96
Risk-Aversion	σ	1
Elasticity of Substitution Between Domestic and Imported Food	ρ^f	0.01
Elasticity of Substitution Between Tradables and Non-Tradables	ρ^o	0.01
Technology		
Land Share in Agriculture Production	α^{la}	0.49
Intermediary Share in Agriculture Production	α^{ma}	0.4
Land Relative Size	l^1/l^2	5
Intermediary Share in Commodity Exporter Sector	α^r	0.75
Capital Share in Tradables Production	α^x	0.44
Physical Capital Share	α^e	0.36
Capital Share in Non-tradables Production	α^n	0.33
Capital Share in Energy Production	α^y	0.33
Depreciation Rate	δ	0.06
Population Share		
Skilled Urban Population Share	$\mu^{urb,s}$	0.31
Unskilled Urban Population Share	$\mu^{urb,u}$	0.19
Rural Population Share	μ^{rur}	0.37
Government Workers Share	μ^{gov}	0.06
Entrepreneur Share	μ^{ent}	0.05

Source: IMF staff.

References

Adams, Richard H., and John Page. 2005. "Do International Migration and Remittances Reduce Poverty in Developing Countries?" *World Development* Volume 33 (10): 1645–69.

African Development Bank, International Monetary Fund, and World Bank Group (AfDB, IMF, and WBG). 2017. "The G-20 Compact with Africa." G-20 Finance Ministers and Central Bank Governors Meeting, March 17–18.

African Development Bank (ADB). 2019. "African Union Commission Calls for Further Financial Input for the NEPAD-IPPF Special Fund." African Development Bank Group. Addis Ababa. July 5. Available at https://www.afdb.org/en/news-and-events/press-releases/african-union-commission-calls-further-financial-input-nepad-ippf-special-fund-24436.

Agler, Ellen. 2019. "Why Philanthropy For – and by – Africans is the Future." World Economic Forum, available at https://www.weforum.org/agenda/2019/08/why-philanthropy-for-and-by-africans-is-the-future/.

Akitoby, Bernadin, Jiro Honda, Hiroaki Miyamoto, Keyra Primus, and Mouhamadou Sy, 2019. "Case Studies in Tax Revenue Mobilization in Low-Income Countries." IMF Working Paper 19/104, International Monetary Fund, Washington, DC.

Andres, Luis, J. Luis Guasch, Thomas Haven, and Vivien Foster. 2008. *The Impact of Private Sector Participation in Infrastructure. Lights, Shadows and the Road Ahead.* World Bank, Washington, DC.

Araya, Gonzalo, Jordan Schwartz, and Luis Andres. 2013. "The Effects of Country Risk and Conflict on Infrastructure PPPs." Policy Research Working Paper No. 6569. World Bank, Washington, DC.

Asian Development Bank (ADB). 2000. Developing Best Practices for Promoting Private Sector Investment in Infrastructure: Roads." Asian Development Bank, Manilla.

Attridge, Samantha, and Lars Engen. 2019. "Blended Finance in the Poorest Countries. The Need for a Better Approach." ODI Report.

African Private Equity and Venture Capital Association (AVCA). 2013. "New Index for African Private Equity Reveals 11% Annualized Returns for 10 Years Ending September 2012." African Private Equity and Venture Association.

African Private Equity and Venture Capital Association (AVCA). 2019. "Profile of Africa's Institutional Investors." African Private Equity and Venture Association.

African Private Equity and Venture Capital Association (AVCA). 2020a. "African Private Equity Industry Survey." African Private Equity and Venture Association.

African Private Equity and Venture Capital Association (AVCA). 2020b. "2019 H1 African Private Equity Data Tracker." African Private Equity and Venture Association.

Barhoumi, Karim, Ha Vu, Shirin Nikaein Towfighian, and Rodolfo Maino. 2018. "Public Investment Efficiency in Sub-Saharan African Countries What Lies Ahead?" IMF African Department Paper 18/09. International Monetary Fund, Washington, DC.

Banerji, Angana, Valerio Crispolti, Era Dabla-Norris, Romain Duval, Christian Ebeke, Davide Furceri, Takuji Komatsuzaki, and Tigran Poghosyan. 2017. "Labor and Product Market Reforms in Advanced Economies: Fiscal Costs, Gains, and Support." IMF Staff Discussion Note 17/03. International Monetary Fund, Washington, DC.

Benedek, Dora, Edward Gemayel, Abdelhak Senhadji, and Alexander F. Tieman. 2021. "A Post-Pandemic Assessment of the Sustainable Development Goals." IMF Staff Discussion Note SDN/2021/003.

Blanc-Brude, Fréderic, Timothy Whittaker, and Simon Wilde. 2017. "Searching for a Listed Infrastructure Asset Class Using Mean–Variance Spanning." *Financial Markets and Portfolio Management* 31: 137–79.

Blended Finance Taskforce and Business and Sustainable Development Commission (BFT BSDC). 2018. "Who is the Private Sector? Key Considerations for Mobilizing Institutional Capital Through Blended Finance." Working Paper.

Bova, Elva, Marta Ruiz-Arranz, Frederik Toscani, and H. Elif Ture. 2016. "The Fiscal Costs of Contingent Liabilities: A New Dataset." IMF Working Paper 16/14. International Monetary Fund, Washington, DC.

Broadband Commission. 2019. "Connecting Africa Through Broadband: A strategy for doubling connectivity by 2021 and reaching universal access by 2030." Broadband Commission for Sustainable Development.

Brocklebank, Peter. 2014. "Private Sector Involvement in Road Financing." Working Paper No. 102. SSATP Africa Transport Policy Program. World Bank, Washington, DC.

Butler, Ryan, and Eunil Lee. 2013. "Fundamentals of Public-Private Partnerships in the Transportation Sector: International Methodologies of Highway Public-private Partnerships and a Framework to Increase the Probability of Success and Allocate Risk." Center for Real Estate, Massachusetts Institute of Technology, Cambridge, MA.

Cambridge Associates. 2020a. "Private Equity and Venture Capital Impact Investing: Index and Benchmark Statistics, March 31, 2020." Cambridge Associates, Boston, MA.

Cambridge Associates. 2020b. "Ex US Private Equity and Venture Capital: Index and Benchmark Statistics, December 31, 2019." Cambridge Associates, Boston, MA.

Cambridge Associates. 2020c. "Private Equity: Index and Benchmark Statistics, December 31, 2019." Cambridge Associates, Boston, MA.

Cambridge Associates. 2020d. "US Venture Capital: Index and Benchmark Statistics, December 31, 2019." Cambridge Associates, Boston, MA.

Capgemini. 2019. *World Wealth Report 2019.* The Wealth Reports, France. Available on https://worldwealthreport.com/resources/world-wealth-report-2020/

Çelik, Serdar, and Mats Isaksson. 2014. "Institutional Investors and Ownership Engagement." *OECD Journal: Financial Market Trends* 2013/2. Available on https://doi.org/10.1787/fmt-2013-5jz734pwtrkc.

Chami, Ralph, Connel Fullenkamp, and Samir Jahjah. 2005. "Are Immigrant Remittance Flows a Source of Capital for Development?" IMF Working Paper 03/189. International Monetary Fund, Washington, DC.

Chao Emmanuel James, Priscilla Serwaah, Prince Baah-Peprah, and Rotem Shneor. 2020. "Crowdfunding in Africa: Opportunities and Challenges." In *Advances in Crowdfunding, Research and Practice*, edited by Rotem Shneor, Liang Zhao, and Bjorn-Tore Flåten. Palgrave Macmillan.

Cherif, Reda, and Fuad Hasanov. 2019. "The Return of the Policy That Shall Not Be Named: Principles of Industrial Policy." IMF Working Paper 19/74. International Monetary Fund, Washington, DC.

Coady, David, Robert Gillingham, Rolando Ossowski, John Piotrowski, Shamsuddin Tareq, and Justin Tyson. 2010. "Petroleum Product Subsidies: Costly, Inequitable, and Rising." IMF Staff Position Note 10/05. International Monetary Fund, Washington, DC.

Coady, David, Javier Arze del Granado, Luc Eyraud, Hui Jin, Vimal Thakoor, Anita Tuladhar, and Lilla Nemeth. 2012. "Automatic Fuel Pricing Mechanisms with Price Smoothing: Design, Implementation, and Fiscal Implications." IMF Technical Notes and Manuals 12/03. International Monetary Fund, Washington, DC.

Coady, David, Valentina Flamini, and Louis Sears. 2015. "The Unequal Benefits of Fuel Subsidies Revisited: Evidence for Developing Countries." IMF Working Paper 15/250. International Monetary Fund, Washington, DC.

Coady, David, Ian Parry, Nghia-Piotr Le, and Baoping Shang. 2019. "Global Fossil Fuel Subsidies Remain Large: An Update Based on Country-Level Estimates." IMF Working Paper 19/89. International Monetary Fund, Washington, DC.

Collier, Paul. 2014. "Attracting International Private Finance for African Infrastructure." *Journal of African Trade* 1: 37–44.

Collier, Paul, and Colin Mayer. 2014. "Unlocking Private Finance for African Infrastructure." available at https://novafrica.org/wp-content/uploads/2015/06/Paul-Collier.pdf.

Collier, Paul, Jonathan Leape, Richard Manning, Colin Mayer, and Staci Warden. 2014. "Private Investment in Infrastructure." Summary of Working-Group Recommendations and Potential Next Steps following the London Roundtable, 27th February, 2014. Available at https://www.oecd.org/daf/inv/investment-policy/2014-AfDB-OECD-Seminar-paper-IGC.pdf

Della Croce, Raffaele, and Juan Yermo. 2013. "Institutional Investors and Infrastructure Financing." OECD Working Papers on Finance, Insurance and Private Pensions, No. 36. OECD Publishing, Paris.

Deloitte. 2014. "Project Bonds: An Alternative Source of Financing Infrastructure Projects." Available at https://www2.deloitte.com/za/en/pages/finance/articles/project-bonds-an-alternative-to-financing-infrastructure-projects.html

Deloitte. 2019. "2018 Deloitte Africa Private Equity Confidence Survey." Available at https://www2.deloitte.com/content/dam/Deloitte/

za/Documents/finance/za_Deloitte-Africa-Private-Equity-Confidence-Survey-2018.pdf

Deutsche Asset Management. 2017. "Why Invest in Infrastructure?" Research Report, May.

Dupoux, Patrick, Tawfik Hammoud, and Seddik El Fihri. 2016. "Why Africa Remains Ripe for Private Equity." The Boston Consulting Group. Available at file:///home/flaayLKC/Downloads/BCG-Why-Africa-Remains-Ripe-for-Private-Equity-Sep-2016_tcm9-149409.pdf.

Eberhard, Anton, Joel Kolker, and James Leighland. 2014. "South Africa's Renewable Energy IPP Procurement Program: Success Factors and Lessons." Public-Private Infrastructure Advisory Facility, Washington DC.

EDHEC. 2017. "Investor Perceptions of Infrastructure, 2017." A Publication of the EDHEC Infrastructure Institute-Singapore. November.

Ehlers, Torsten. 2014. "Understanding the Challenges for Infrastructure Finance." Bank for International Settlements Working Paper No. 454. Basel.

Emerging Markets Private Equity Association (EMPEA). 2018. "The Road Ahead for African Private Equity." Washington, DC.

Energy Sector Management Assistance Program (ESMAP). 2015. "Private Sector Participation in Electricity Transmission and Distribution: Experiences from Brazil, Peru, The Philippines, and Turkey." Knowledge Series 023/15, Energy Sector Management Assistance Program.

Energy Sector Management Assistance Program (ESMAP). 2019. "Mini Grids for Half a Billion People: Market Outlook and Handbook for Decision Makers." Energy Sector Management Assistance Program (ESMAP) Technical Report 014/19. World Bank, Washington, DC.

Ernst & Young, and African Private Equity and Venture Association (EY & AVCA). 2018. "How Private Equity Investors Create Value." Ernst Young and African Private Equity and Venture Association.

Estache, Antonio, and Caroline Philippe. 2012. "The Impact of Private Participation in Infrastructure in Developing Countries: Taking Stock of About 20 Years of Experience." ECARES Working Paper 2012–043.

Estache, Antonio, Tomas Serebrisky, and Liam Wern-Lewis. 2015. "Financing Infrastructure in Developing Countries." *Oxford Review of Economic Policy* 31 (3–4): 279–304.

Estrin, Saul, and Adeline Pelletier. 2018. "Privatization in Developing Countries: What Are the Lessons of Recent Experience?" *The World Bank Research Observer.*

European Bank for Reconstruction and Development (EBRD). 2018. "Additionality in the EBRD – Review of Concept and Application." March 2018 EBRD Evaluation Department, SS17–107.

Farquharson, Edward, Clemencia Torres de Mästle, E. R. Yescombe, and Javier Encinas. 2011. "How to Engage with the Private Sector in Public-Private Partnerships in Emerging Markets." Public-Private Infrastructure Advisory Facility and the World Bank, Washington, DC.

Flanigan, Shawn Teresa. 2017. "Crowdfunding and Diaspora Philanthropy: An Integration of the Literature and Major Concepts." *Voluntas: International Journal of Voluntary and Nonprofit Organizations* 28 (2): 492–509.

Foundation Center and Council on Foundations. 2018. *The State of Global Giving by US Foundations: 2011–2015.* Available on https://www.cof.org/content/state-global-giving-us-foundations-2011-2015

Foster, Vivien, and Cecilia Briceño-Garmendia. Eds. 2010. *Africa's Infrastructure A Time for Transformation.* Paris and Washington, DC: Agence Française de Développement and the World Bank.

Foster, Vivien, Samantha Witte, Sudeshna Ghosh Banerjee, and Alejandro Moreno. 2017. "Charting the Diffusion of Power Sector Reforms across the Developing World." Policy Research Working Paper 8235. World Bank, Washington, DC.

Foster, Vivien, and Anshul Rana. 2020. "Rethinking Power Sector Reform in the Developing World." *Sustainable Infrastructure Series.* World Bank, Washington, DC.

Gates, Bill, and Melinda Gates. 2020. "Reflecting on the First Two Decades of our Foundation." 2020 Annual Letter. Available at https://www.gatesnotes.com/2020-Annual-Letter?WT.tBGEM

Gaspar, Vitor, David Amaglobeli, Mercedes Garcia-Escribano, Delphine Prady, and Mauricio Soto. 2019. "Fiscal Policy and Development: Human, Social, and Physical Investment for the SDGs." IMF Staff Discussion Note 19/02. International Monetary Fund, Washington, DC.

Gassner, Katharina, Alexander Popov, and Nataliya Pushak. 2009. "Does Private Sector Participation Improve Performance in Electricity and Water Distribution?" Trends and Policy Options No. 6. World Bank, Washington, DC.

Gianoncelli, Alessia, Gianluca Gaggiotti, Priscilla Boiardiand, and Arnau Picón Martínez. 2019 "15 Years of Impact—Taking Stock and Looking Ahead." European Venture Philanthropy Association.

Global Impact Investing Network (GIIN). 2018. "2018 Annual Impact Investor Survey." Global Impact Investing Network, New York.

Global Impact Investing Network (GIIN). 2019. "2019 Annual Impact Investor Survey." Global Impact Investing Network, New York.

Global Impact Investing Network (GIIN). 2020. "2020 Annual Impact Investor Survey." Global Impact Investing Network, New York.

Global Infrastructure Hub (GIH). 2018. "Leading Practices in Governmental Processes Facilitating Infrastructure Project Preparation." Available at file:///C:/Mission%20September%20October%202019/SDG%20project/Bankability/Project%20Preparation%20GIH.pdf.

Global Sustainable Investment Alliance (GSIA). 2019. "Global Sustainable Investment Review for 2018." Washington, DC.

Gordon, K. 2008. "Investment Guarantees and Political Risk Insurance: Institutions, Incentives and Development." OECD Investment Policy Perspectives 2008.

Group of Twenty (G20). 2017. "The G20 Compact with Africa, A Joint AfDB, IMF and WBG Report." Baden-Baden. Available at https://www.compactwithafrica.org/content/dam/Compact%20with%20Africa/2017-03-30-g20-compact-with-africa-report.pdf.

Group of Twenty (G20). 2018. *Roadmap to Infrastructure as an Asset Class.* G20 Argentina 2018. Available at https://www.oecd.org/g20/roadmap_to_infrastructure_as_an_asset_class_argentina_presidency_1_0.pdf

Group of Twenty Infrastructure Working Group (G20 IWG). 2018. G20 Principles for the Infrastructure Project Preparation Phase." Available at https://www.gihub.org/project-preparation/.

Graduate School of Business University of Cape Town (GSB). 2020. "The African Investing for Impact Barometer." Bertha Centre. UCT Graduate Scholle of Business.

Guasch, J. Luis. 2004. "Granting and Renegotiating Infrastructure Concessions Doing it Right." WBI Development Studies, World Bank Institute 28816.

Gupta, Sanjeev, Catherine Pattillo, and Smita Wagh. 2007. "Impact of Remittances on Poverty and Financial Development in Sub-Saharan Africa." IMF Working Paper 07/38. International Monetary Fund, Washington, DC.

Gupta, Poonam, and Olivier Masetti. 2018. "Capital Flow Measures. Structural or Cyclical Policy Tools?" World Bank Policy Research Working Paper 8418. World Bank, Washington, DC.

Harris, Clive. 2003. "Private Participation in Infrastructure in Developing Countries. Trends, Impacts and Policy Lessons." World Bank Working Paper 5. World Bank, Washington, DC.

Hausmann, Ricardo, Dani Rodrik, and Andrés. Velasco. 2006. "Getting the Diagnosis Right." *Finance & Development* 43 (1).

Hemming, Richard. 2006. "Public-Private Partnerships, Government Guarantees, and Fiscal Risk." IMF Special Issues. International Monetary Fund, Washington, DC.

Hertzmark, Donald. 2008. "Private Sector Participation in the Power Sector." USAID and National Association of Regulatory Utility Commissioners.

ICA. 2018. "Infrastructure Financing Trends in Africa – 2018". The Infrastructure Consortium for Africa Secretariat c/o African Development Bank. Abidjan.

Independent Evaluation Group (IEG). 2008. "Independent Evaluation of IFC's Development Results 2008: IFC's Additionality in Supporting Private Sector Development." International Finance Corporation.

Inderst, Georg. 2009. "Pension Fund Investment in Infrastructure." OECD Working Papers on Insurance and Private Pensions, No. 32, OECD Publishing. OECD, Paris.

Inderst, Georg, and Fiona Stewart. 2014. "Institutional Investment in Infrastructure in Emerging Markets and Developing Economies." PPIAF, World Bank Group.

International Finance Corporation (IFC). 2018a. "Private Equity and Venture Capital's Role in Catalyzing Sustainable Investment. Input Paper for the G-20 Sustainable Finance Study Group." International Finance Corporation.

International Finance Corporation (IFC). 2018b. "IFC SME Ventures: Investing in Private Equity in Sub-Saharan African Fragile and Conflict-Affected Situations". International Finance Corporation, World Bank Group, Washington, DC.

International Monetary Fund (IMF). 2004. "Public-Private Partnerships." IMF Policy Paper available at https://www.imf.org/external/np/fad/2004/pifp/eng/031204.htm

International Monetary Fund (IMF). 2012. "The Liberalization and Management of Capital Flows: An Institutional View." IMF Policy Paper available at https://www.imf.org/en/Publications/Policy-Papers/Issues/2016/12/31/The-Liberalization-and-Management-of-Capital-Flows-An-Institutional-View-PP4720

International Monetary Fund (IMF). 2013a. "Guidance Note for the Liberalization and Management of Capital Flows." International Monetary Fund, Washington, DC.

International Monetary Fund (IMF). 2013b. "Energy Subsidy Reform—Lessons and Implications." IMF Policy Paper. International Monetary Fund, Washington, DC.

International Monetary Fund (IMF). 2014. "Is It Time for an Infrastructure Push? The Macroeconomic Effects of Public Investment." Chapter 3, *World Economic Outlook,* Washington, DC, October.

International Monetary Fund (IMF). 2015a. "Options for Low Income Countries' Effective and Efficient Use of Tax Incentives for Investment." IMF Policy Paper. International Monetary Fund, Washington, DC.

International Monetary Fund (IMF). 2015b. "Evolving Monetary Policy Frameworks in Low-Income and Other Developing Countries." Staff Report. International Monetary Fund, Washington DC.

International Monetary Fund (IMF). 2016a. "Macroeconomic Developments and prospects in Low Income and Developing Countries—2016." IMF Policy Paper. International Monetary Fund, Washington, DC.

International Monetary Fund (IMF). 2016b. "Revised Guidelines for Foreign Exchange Reserve Management." International Monetary Fund, Washington, DC.

International Monetary Fund (IMF). 2016c. "Guidance Note on the Assessment of Reserve Adequacy and Related Considerations." International Monetary Fund, Washington, DC.

International Monetary Fund (IMF). 2016d. "Capital Flows—Review of Experience with the Institutional View." IMF Policy Paper available at https://www.imf.org/en/Publications/Policy-Papers/Issues/2017/01/13/PP5081-Capital-Flows-Review-of-Experience-with-the-Institutional-View

International Monetary Fund (IMF). 2017. "Economic Diversification in Sub-Saharan Africa." Chapter 3 of the *Regional Economic Outlook: Sub-Saharan Africa.* Washington, DC, October.

International Monetary Fund (IMF). 2018a. "Private Investment to Reinvigorate Growth." Chapter 3 of *Regional Economic Outlook: Sub-Saharan Africa.* Washington, DC, April.

International Monetary Fund (IMF). 2018b. "Macroeconomic Developments and Prospects in Low-Income Developing Countries—2018." International Monetary Fund, Washington, DC.

International Monetary Fund (IMF). 2018c. "Domestic Revenue Mobilization in Sub-Saharan Africa: What Are the Possibilities?" Chapter 3, *Regional Economic Outlook: Sub-Saharan Africa,* Washington, DC, April.

International Monetary Fund (IMF). 2019a. "Fintech in Sub-Saharan African Countries: A Game Changer?" African Departmental Paper. International Monetary Fund, Washington, DC.

International Monetary Fund (IMF). 2019b. "Sustainable Development, Sustainable Debt: Finding the Right Balance." Conference Paper prepared by an IMF staff team led by Dominique Desruelle, Ivo Razafimahefa, and Cemile Sancak. Available at https://www.imf.org/en/News/Seminars/Conferences/2019/12/02/sustainable-development-and-debt.

International Monetary Fund (IMF). 2019c. "Institutional Investors. Falling Rates, Rising Risks." Chapter 3, *Global Financial Stability Report: Lower for Longer*. Washington, DC, October.

International Monetary Fund (IMF). 2019d. "Public Investment Management Assessment (PIMA). Strengthening Infrastructure Governance." IMF Fiscal Affairs Department. International Monetary Fund, Washington, DC.

International Monetary Fund (IMF). 2019e. ""Sustainable Finance" Chapter 6, *Global Financial Stability Report*. Washington, DC, October.

International Monetary Fund (IMF). 2020. "Adapting to Climate Change in Sub-Saharan Africa." Chapter 2, *Regional Economic Outlook: Sub-Saharan Africa*. Washington, DC, April.

International Monetary Fund (IMF), and World Bank. 2019. "PPP Fiscal Risk Assessment Model, PFRAM 2.0" Use Manual, September 2019. International Monetary Fund, Washington, DC.

Irwin, Tim. 2003. "Public Money for Private Infrastructure—Deciding When to Offer Guarantees, Output-Based Subsidies, and Other Fiscal Support." World Bank, Washington, DC.

Irwin, Tim, Samah Mazraani, and Sandeep Saxena. 2018. "How to Control the Costs of Public-Private Partnerships." IMF How To Notes 18/04. International Monetary Fund, Washington, DC.

Jaffe, Adam B. 1998. "The Importance of "Spillovers" in the Policy Mission of the Advanced Technology Program." *The Journal of Technology Transfer* 23: 11–19.

Jahan, Sarwat, and Daili Wang. 2016. "Capital Account Openness in Low-income Developing Countries: Evidence from a New Database." IMF Working Paper 16/252. International Monetary Fund, Washington, DC.

Jerome, Afeikhena. 2008. "Private Sector Participation in Infrastructure in Africa." African Peer Review Mechanism Secretariat.

Juvonen, Katja, Arun Kumar, Hassen Ben Ayed, and Antonio Ocana Marin. 2019. "Unleashing the Potential of Institutional Investors in

Africa." Working Paper Series N°325, African Development Bank, Abidjan, Côte d'Ivoire.

Kapoor, Sony. 2019. "Billions to Trillions—A Reality Check. Blending: Development Finance Institutions and Financing the Sustainable Development Goals." A RE-DEFINE Policy Brief for Stamp Out Poverty.

Kappel, Birte Pfeiffer, and Helmut Reisen. 2017." Fostering Private Long-Term Investment in Africa." Compact with Africa. German Development Institute Discussion Paper 13/2017. Bonn.

Karacadag, Cem, V. Sundararajan, and Jennifer Elliott. 2003. "Managing Risks in Financial Market Development: The Role of Sequencing." IMF Working Paper 03/116. International Monetary Fund, Washington, DC.

Kortekaas, Brendon. 2015. "Infrastructure Finance in the Developing World. Infrastructure Pipeline and Need for Robust Project Preparation." Working Paper Series, The Global Green Growth Institute and The Intergovernmental Group of Twenty-Four on Monetary Affairs and Development (G-24). Soul and Washington, DC.

Laeven, Luc. 2014. "The Development of Local Capital Markets: Rationale and Challenges." IMF Working Paper 14/234. International Monetary Fund, Washington, DC.

Lagomarsino, Gina, Stefan Nachuk, and Sapna Singh Kundra. 2009. "Public Stewardship of Private Providers in Mixed Health Systems." Synthesis Report from the Rockefeller Foundation–Sponsored Initiative on the Role of the Private Sector in Health Systems in Developing Countries. Washington, DC.

Leigland, James. 2018. "Public-Private Partnerships in Developing Countries: The Emerging Evidence-Based Critique." *The World Bank Research Observer* 33 (1).

Lewis, Laura. 2013. "Is There a Role for the Private Sector in Education?" Education for Global Development, World Bank, Washington, DC.

Lusk-Stover, Oni, and Harry Anthony Patrinos. 2015. "Education for All: The Private Sector Can Contribute." Private Sector and Development, World Bank, Washington, DC.

Maury, Frédéric, and Amaury de Féligonde. 2019. "African Logistics: Time for Revolution." Africa CEO Forum/Orkan.

Mayaki, Ibrahim. 2019. "Why is the Proper Structuring of Major Infrastructure Projects in Africa a Priority?" AU-PIDA. 2019. Available at https://www.au-pida.org/news/why-is-the-proper-structuring-of-major-infrastructure-projects-in-africa-a-priority .

Menzies, Iain, and Cledan Mandri-Perrott. 2010. "Private Sector Participation in Urban Rail: Getting the Structure Right." *Gridlines*, Note no. 54, April 2010, Public-Private Infrastructure Advisory Facility, World Bank, Washington, DC.

McKinsey & Company. 2020. "A New Decade for Private Markets." McKinsey Global Private Markets Review 2020. February.

Mercer LLC. 2018. "Investment in African Infrastructure, Challenges and Opportunities." September 2018.

Mittal, Abhishek. 2020. "Low Returns: How African Private Equity Needs to Change Its Approach." published in *How We Made It in Africa* and available at https://www.howwemadeitinafrica.com/low-returns-how-african-private-equity-needs-to-change-its-approach/64190/

Mlachila, Montfort, Larry Cui, Ahmat Jidoud, Monique Newiak, Bozena Radzewicz-Bak, Misa Takebe, Yanmin Ye, and Jiayi Zhang. 2016. "Financial Development in Sub-Saharan Africa." African Department Paper. International Monetary Fund, Washington, DC.

Moody's Investors Service. (2020a). "Default and Recovery Rates for Project Finance Bank Loans, 1983–2018." Moody's Investor Service. Infrastructure and Project Finance, March 9, 2020.

Moody's Investors Service. (2020b). "Infrastructure default and recovery rates, 1983–2019." Moody's Investor Service. Infrastructure and Project Finance, October 9, 2020.

Moyo, Bhekikosi. 2010. "Philanthropy in Africa: Functions, Status, Challenges and Opportunities." In *Global Philanthropy*, edited by N. MacDonald, and L. de Borms. London: MF Publishing.

Moyo, Bhekikosi. 2017. "The Infrastructure for Philanthropy in Africa: Developments, Challenges and Opportunities." In *Infrastructure in Focus: A New Global Picture of Organizations Serving Philanthropy – Growing and Strengthening the Field,* edited by B. Knight and P. Ribeiro. Worldwide Initiative for Grantmaker Support.

Newell, Graeme, Hsu Wen Peng, and Anthony De Francesco. 2011. "The Performance of Unlisted Infrastructure in Investment Portfolios." *Journal of Property Research* 28 (1).

Nonnemberg, Marcelo Braga, and Mario Jorge Cardoso de Mendonça. 2004. "The Determinants of Foreign Direct Investment in Developing Countries." Proceedings of the 32nd Brazilian Economics Meeting. Brazilian Association of Graduate Programs in Economics. Available at https://ideas.repec.org/p/anp/en2004/061.html#download.

Oberholzer, Basil, Katharina Schneider-Roos, Charlotte Boulanger, and Maryke van Staden. 2018. "Summary of Good Practice of Successful Project Preparation Facilities." Global Infrastructure Basel (GIB) and Deutsche Gesellschaft für Internationale Zusammenarbeit (GIZ) GmbH. Basel, Eschenbach.

O'Neill, Phillip. 2009. "Infrastructure Investment and the Management of Risk." In *Managing Financial Risks: From Global to Local*, edited by Gordon L. Clark, Adam D. Dixon, and Ashby H. B. Monk. Oxford University Press.

Organisation for Economic Co-operation and Development (OECD). 2008. *Public-Private Partnerships: In Pursuit of Risk Sharing and Value for Money.* Paris.

Organisation for Economic Co-operation and Development (OECD). 2009. "Private Sector Participation in Water Infrastructure: OECD Checklist for Public Action." Paris.

Organisation for Economic Co-operation and Development (OECD). 2012. "Mapping Support for Africa's Infrastructure Investment." OECD Aid for Investment in Africa's Infrastructure Project. Paris.

Organisation for Economic Co-operation and Development (OECD). 2014. "Pooling of Institutional Investors Capital—Selected Case Studies in Unlisted Equity Infrastructure." Paris.

Organisation for Economic Co-operation and Development (OECD). 2015. Infrastructure Financing Instruments and Incentives. OECD Report. Paris.

Organisation for Economic Co-operation and Development (OECD). 2017a. "Pension Markets in Focus No. 14." Available at https://www.oecd.org/pensions/private-pensions/pensionmarketsinfocus.htm

Organisation for Economic Co-operation and Development (OECD). 2017b. *Interrelations between Public Policies, Migration and Development.* OECD Publishing, Paris. Available at http://dx.doi.org/10.1787/9789264265615-en

Organisation for Economic Co-operation and Development (OECD). 2018. "Private Philanthropy for Development, The Development Dimension." OECD Publishing, Paris.

Organisation for Economic Co-operation and Development (OECD). 2019a. "Certifying Reform Efforts Through International Standards for Compact with Africa Countries. " OECD Background Paper prepared for the AfDB-IMF-OECD-WBG workshop on international standards for Compact and G20 countries, November 4–5, 2019. Paris.

Organisation for Economic Co-operation and Development (OECD). 2019b. "Annual Survey of Large Pension Funds and Public Pension Reserve Funds." Available at www.oecd.org/finance/survey-large-pension-funds.htm.

Organisation for Economic Co-operation and Development (OECD). 2020a. "OECD Institutional Investors Statistics 2020." OECD Publishing, Paris. Available at https://doi.org/10.1787/9a827fb7-en.

Organisation for Economic Co-operation and Development (OECD). 2020b. OECD Global Pensions Statistics. Available at www.oecd.org/daf/pensions/gps

Organisation for Economic Co-operation and Development (OECD). 2020c. "OECD Annual Survey of Investment Regulation of Pension Funds and Other Pension Providers." Paris.

Organisation for Economic Co-operation and Development (OECD). 2020d. *Private philanthropy for the SDGs Insights from the Latest OECD DAC Statistics*. Available at https://www.oecd.org/development/financing-sustainable-development/development-finance-standards/beyond-oda-foundations.htm

OECD netFWD. 2014. "Venture Philanthropy in Development: Dynamics, Challenges and Lessons in the Search for Greater Impact." OECD Development Centre, Paris.

OECD netFWD. 2017. "Bringing Foundations and Governments Closer: Evidence from Kenya." OECD Development Centre, Paris.

Peterhoff, Daniela, Paul Calvey, Quinton Goddard, Siobhan Cleary, and Stefano Alderighi. 2016. "Enhancing Liquidity in Emerging Markets Exchanges." Oliver Wyman and World Federation of Exchanges. Available at www.oliverwyman.com/content/dam/oliver-wyman/global/en/2016/oct/Liquidity-in-Emerging-Markets-Exchanges-.pdf.

Power Futures South Africa. 2019. "Unbundling Update: Understanding Proposed Reforms in South Africa."

Preqin. 2016. "Special Report: The Infrastructure Market in Africa." Preqin Alternative Assets Intelligent Data.

Preqin. 2020a. Preqin Global Infrastructure Report. London.

Preqin. 2020b. Preqin Investor Outlook: Alternative Assets H1 2020. London.

Principles for Responsible Investment (PRI). 2020a. "A Blueprint for Responsible Investment." PRI in partnership with UNEP Finance Initiative, United Nations and Global Compact.

Principles for Responsible Investment (PRI). 2020b. Dataset on PRI Growth 2006–2020. Available at https://www.unpri.org/pri

Private Equity International (PEI). 2020. "Africa. Mapping Out the Continent's Hotspots." September 2020. Available at https://www.privateequityinternational.com/download-peis-special-report-on-africa/

Rall, Jamie, James B. Reed, and Nicholas J. Farber. 2010. "Public-Private Partnerships for Transportation: A Toolkit for Legislators." National Conference of State Legislators Partners Project on Public Private Partnerships for Transportation.

Razlog, Lilia, Chris Marrison, and Tim Irwin. 2020. "Scenario Analysis Tool for Assessment and Monitoring of Government Guarantees." World Bank Discussion Paper MTI Global Practuce No. 21 May 2020.

Rodrik, Dani. 2004. "Growth Strategies." Harvard University.

Rojas-Suarez, Liliana. 2014. "Towards Strong and Stable Capital Markets in Emerging Market Economies." BIS Paper 75, Bank for International Settlements, Basel, Switzerland.

Romero, María José. 2015. "What Lies Beneath? A Critical Assessment of PPPs and Their Impact on Sustainable Development." Eurodad.

Rutzen, Douglas. 2015. "Aid Barriers and the Rise of Philanthropic Protectionism." *International Journal of Not-for-Profit Law* 17 (1).

Sachs, Jeffrey and Guido Schmidt-Traub. 2017. "Global Fund lessons for Sustainable Development Goals: Transparency and independence underpin successes," *Science* 356 (6333): 32–33.

Sahay, Ratna, Martin Čihák, Papa N'Diaye, Adolfo Barajas, Ran Bi, Diana Ayala, Yuan Gao, Annette Kyobe, Lam Nguyen, Christian Saborowski, Katsiaryna Svirydzenka, and Seyed Reza Yousefi. 2015. "Rethinking Financial Deepening: Stability and Growth in Emerging Markets." IMF Staff Discussion Note 15/08. International Monetary Fund, Washington, DC.

Saxena, Sandeep. 2017. "How to Strengthen the Management of Government Guarantees." IMF How-to Note. International Monetary Fund, Washington, DC.

Schiff, Hannah, and Hannah Dithrich. 2018. "Lasting Impact: The Need For Responsible Exits." The Global Impact Investors Network. New York.

Schlapinski, Jeff. 2018. "EMPEA Brief: The Road Ahead for African Private Equity. Emerging Markets Private Equity Association. Available at https://www.empea.org/app/uploads/2018/05/EMPEA-Briefs_Africa_FINAL_WEB.pdf.

Sha, Mumtaz Hussain. 2016. "The Effect of Macroeconomic Stability on Inward FDI in African Developing Countries." *International Journal of Business Studies Review* 1 (1). Available at https://mpra.ub.uni-muenchen.de/82014/1/MPRA_paper_82014.pdf.

Schwier, Jan, Craig Wallington, Maddie Holland, and Wendy Magoronga. 2020. "The Landscape of Large-Scale Giving by African Philanthropists." A research brief by the Bridgespan Group.

Sulser, Patricia. 2018. "Infrastructure PPPs in the Most Challenging Developing Countries: Closing the Gap." IFLR.

Sy, Amadou, Rodolfo Maino, Alexander Massara, Hector Perez-Saiz, and Preya Sharma. 2019. "FinTech in Sub-Saharan African Countries: A Game Changer?" Departmental Paper 19/04. International Monetary Fund, Washington, DC.

Tyson, Judith. 2018. "Private Infrastructure Financing in Developing Countries. Five Challenges, Five Solutions." ODI Working Paper 536. World Economic Forum, Geneva, Switzerland.

United Nations (UN). 2018. "Financing for Development: Progress and Prospects 2018." Report of the Inter-agency Task Force on Financing for Development, United Nations. Geneva, Switzerland.

United Nations (UN). 2019. "SDG Bonds: Leveraging Capital Markets for the SDGs" Prepared by the UN Global Compact Action Platform on Financial Innovation for the SDGs. Geneva, Switzerland.

United Nations Conference on Trade and Development (UNCTAD). 2019. "World Investment Report 2019." United Nations, Geneva, Switzerland.

United Nations Development Programme (UNDP). 2015. "Impact Investment in Africa: Trends, Constraints & Opportunities." United Nations Development Program, Geneva, Switzerland.

United States Agency for International Development (USAID). 2016. "Project Preparation Facilities Toolbox." Power Africa, A US Government-led Partnership. USAID, April 2016. Available at https://2012-2017.usaid.gov/sites/default/files/documents/1860/PPF%20Toolbox%20REVISED.pdf.

United States Department of Transportation (USDT). 2016. "Guidebook on Financing of Highway Public-Private Partnership Projects." Available at https://www.fhwa.dot.gov/ipd/p3/toolkit/publications/other_guides/financing_of_highway_p3_projects/

Wealth-X. 2020. *Billionaire Census 2020*. Available at https://www.wealthx.com/report/the-wealth-x-billionaire-census-2020/

World Bank. 2003a. *Private participation in infrastructure: trends in developing countries in 1990–2001 (English)*. World Bank, Washington, DC.

World Bank. 2003b. "Private Participation in Health Services." *Human Development Network, Health, Nutrition, and Population Series.* World Bank, Washington, DC.

World Bank. 2006a. *Global Economic Prospects Economic Implications of Remittances and Migration.* International Bank for Reconstruction and Development/The World Bank, Washington, DC.

World Bank. 2006b. "Approaches to Private Participation in Water Services: A Toolkit." Public-Private Infrastructure Advisory Facility and the World Bank, Washington, DC.

World Bank. 2010. "Financing Higher Education in Africa." World Bank, Washington, DC.

World Bank. 2011. "Healthy Partnerships: How Governments Can Engage the Private Sector to Improve Health in Africa." World Bank, Washington, DC.

World Bank. 2014. "What Matters Most for Engaging the Private Sector in Education: A Framework Paper." SABER Working Paper Series, Number 8, July 2014. World Bank, Washington, DC.

World Bank. 2016. "The State of PPPs. Infrastructure Public-Private Partnerships in Emerging Markets & Developing Economies 1991–2015." World Bank, Washington, DC.

World Bank. 2017a. "Public-Private Partnerships: Reference Guide Version 3." World Bank, Washington, DC.

World Bank. 2017b. "Africa's Pulse, Spring 2017: Analysis of Issues Shaping Africa's Economic Future (April)." Volume 15. World Bank, Washington, DC.

World Bank. 2017c. "Who Sponsors Infrastructure Projects? Disentangling public and private contributions." World Bank, Washington, DC

World Bank. 2018a. "Contribution of Institutional Investors. Private Investment in Infrastructure 2011-H1 2011." World Bank. Washington, DC.

World Bank. 2018b. "Perspectives of Institutional Investors and Input into the Investor Forum." World Bank. Washington, DC.

World Bank. 2018c. "Investments in IDA Countries. Private Participation in Infrastructure (PPI). 2013–2017." World Bank. Washington, DC.

World Bank. 2020a. "Private Participation in Infrastructure (PPI). 2019. Annual Report." World Bank, Washington, DC.

World Bank. 2020b. "Phase II: COVID-19 Crisis through a Migration Lens Migration and Development Brief 33." October 2020. KNOMAD. World Bank, Washington, DC.

World Economic Forum (WEF). 2016. "Risk Mitigation Instruments in Infrastructure, Gap Analysis." World Economic Forum, Geneva.

World Economic Forum (WEF). 2019. "The Global Competitiveness Report 2019." World Economic Forum, Geneva.

Yescombe, E. R. 2017. "Public-Private Partnerships in Sub-Saharan Africa: Case Studies for Policymakers." Dar es Salaam: UONGOZI Institute.

Zegras, Christopher. 2003. "Private Sector Participation in Urban Transport Infrastructure Provision." Sustainable Transport: A Sourcebook for Policymakers in Developing Cities, Module 1c, Sustainable Urban Transport Project.

Ziegler, Tania, and Rotem Shneor. 2020. "The Global Alternative Finance Benchmarking Report." Cambridge, UK: Cambridge Centre for Alternative Finance.